Sex Discrimination in the Labor Market

Sex Discrimination in the Labor Market

Joni Hersch

Vanderbilt University Law School
131 21st Avenue South
Nashville, TN 37203, USA
joni.hersch@vanderbilt.edu

the essence of knowledge

Boston – Delft

Foundations and Trends® in Microeconomics

Published, sold and distributed by:
now Publishers Inc.
PO Box 1024
Hanover, MA 02339
USA
Tel. +1-781-985-4510
www.nowpublishers.com
sales@nowpublishers.com

Outside North America:
now Publishers Inc.
PO Box 179
2600 AD Delft
The Netherlands
Tel. +31-6-51115274

Library of Congress Control Number: 2006935709

The preferred citation for this publication is J. Hersch, Sex Discrimination in the Labor Market, Foundation and Trends® in Microeconomics, vol 2, no 4, pp 281–361, 2006

Printed on acid-free paper

ISBN: 1-933019-47-6

Foundations and Trends® in Microeconomics

Volume 2 Issue 4, 2006

Editorial Board

Editorial Scope

Foundations and Trends® in Microeconomics publishes survey and tutorial articles in the following topics:

- Environmental Economics
  - Contingent Valuation
  - Environmental Health Risks
  - Climate Change
  - Endangered Species
  - Market-based Policy Instruments
- Health Economics
  - Moral Hazard
  - Medical Care Markets
  - Medical Malpractice
  - Insurance economics
- Industrial Organization
  - Theory of the Firm
  - Regulatory Economics
  - Market Structure
  - Auctions
  - Monopolies and Antitrust
  - Transaction Cost Economics
- Labor Economics
  - Labor Supply
  - Labor Demand
  - Labor Market Institutions
  - Search Theory
  - Wage Structure
  - Income Distribution
  - Race and Gender
- Law and Economics
  - Models of Litigation
  - Crime
  - Torts, Contracts and Property
  - Constitutional Law
- Public Economics
  - Public Goods
  - Environmental Taxation
  - Social Insurance
  - Public Finance
  - International Taxation

Information for Librarians

Foundations and Trends® in Microeconomics, 2006, Volume 2, 6 issues. ISSN paper version 1547-9846. ISSN online version 1547-9854. Also available as a combined paper and online subscription.

Foundations and Trends® in
Microeconomics
Vol. 2, No 4 (2006) 281–361

DOI: 10.1561/0700000007

Sex Discrimination in the Labor Market

Joni Hersch

Vanderbilt University Law School, 131 21st Avenue South, Nashville, TN 37203, USA, joni.hersch@vanderbilt.edu

Abstract

This paper examines sources of gender pay disparity and the factors that contribute to this pay gap. Many researchers question the role of discrimination and instead attribute the residual pay gap to gender differences in preferences. The main issue considered in this paper is whether gender differences in choices, especially with respect to the family and household, are indeed responsible for the gender pay gap, or whether discrimination plays a role. On balance, the evidence indicates that sex discrimination remains a possible explanation of the unexplained gender pay gap. This is consistent with the continuing high profile sex discrimination litigation suggestive of on-going inferior treatment on the basis of sex.

Contents

1

Introduction

Women have made huge advances relative to men in labor force participation, occupational status, and educational attainment. Women now comprise the majority of college students and half of the students in law school and medical school. Yet women continue to earn less than men, and while the gender pay gap has narrowed, a substantial gap remains. This survey article examines sources of this pay disparity and the factors that contribute to women's relative advancement over time. Whether sex discrimination plays a role in the persistent gender pay gap is a topic of considerable debate in academic research as well as in the workplace. Although concerns over discrimination pervaded the debate over sex disparities in pay throughout the 1970s and 1980s, many observers now deny the possibility of discrimination and instead attribute the residual pay gap to gender differences in preferences, especially with respect to balancing market work with family responsibilities. The evidence presented in this survey shows that sex discrimination should not be dismissed as a source of the unexplained gender pay gap.

Arguments that pay gaps arise from choice seem sensible. Theoretical models of discrimination usually show the eventual elimination of discrimination due to market forces. And models of optimal allocation of time within a household imply that gender differences in household and child-related responsibilities will lead men and women to make different choices with respect to the labor market and home, and these choices may result in a gender pay gap. Differences in anticipated and actual labor market commitment and in preferences will lead to gender differences in investment in market-related characteristics, such as education and training, and lesser amounts of market capital will result in lower earnings. Some studies show that the presence of children has a negative effect on women's earnings. Women perform a disproportionate share of housework, and time spent on housework has been shown to have a direct negative impact on wages. Differences in household responsibilities and preferences may also affect other dimensions of labor market outcomes. For instance, women who are primarily responsible for the household may accept employment in jobs that are more compatible with household responsibilities, such as those closer to home, with more flexible work schedules, offering generous maternity leave policies, or with lower levels of injury or fatality job risk. Compensating differentials associated with job characteristics may thereby affect the pay gap.

Hence, it is easy to understand the appeal of choice-based explanations of the gender pay gap. But the empirical evidence is not clear cut. By definition, labor market discrimination is characterized by unequal treatment of equally productive persons in a way that is related to observable characteristics such as sex, race, or ethnicity. The bulk of the literature on sex disparities in the labor market examines whether an unexplained pay disparity remains after controlling for individual characteristics that are expected to influence earnings, with control variables serving as proxies for productivity. Thus, controlling for characteristics that derive from choices of market work relative to family should eliminate an unexplained pay gap. The literature, however, documents gender disparities in pay that persist even with extensive controls for education, actual work experience, training, family characteristics, and so on. Unexplained disparities are often interpreted as due to discrimination. But because there is always the possibility that some unmeasured factor is actually responsible for any unexplained pay disparity, such evidence on the existence or persistence of discrimination is not conclusive.

The main issue considered in this paper is whether gender differences in choices, especially with respect to the family and household, are indeed responsible for the gender pay gap, or whether discrimination plays a role. I begin Section 2 by documenting trends showing considerable convergence of men and women with respect to labor force participation, earnings, and occupational distribution. Sections 3 and 4 discuss measurement and empirical evidence on the unexplained gender pay gap and trends in occupational segregation, respectively. Even with extensive controls for characteristics that affect earnings, a considerable unexplained pay gap remains, and occupational crowding arising from segregation into occupations by sex is unlikely to be an important explanation of the gender pay gap.

Section 5 discusses the role of gender differences in turnover in explaining the pay gap. Notably, there is little difference between men and women in quit rates or in average job tenure. The evidence summarized in this section shows that gender differences in turnover do not explain the gender pay disparity. Section 6 describes evidence on the impact of family and housework on pay. While there is some evidence that the presence of children lowers women's earnings, overall the evidence is mixed, and any effect varies by education and over the life cycle. There is more consistent support for a negative effect of housework time on earnings. However, contrary to popular belief, family and housework are not the major cause of the gender pay gap.

Section 7 looks at whether compensating differentials for attractive working conditions, such as flexible work schedules and safer jobs, explains the gap. Although an appealing explanation, compensating differentials are not responsible for the gender pay gap. Section 8 looks at the role of educational choices, particularly with respect to college major. While there is less segregation by sex in college major now than earlier, controlling for college major does not eliminate the gender pay gap except among new college graduates. Section 9 discusses studies that control for actual productivity, as this approach avoids the omitted-productivity-factor criticism levied at wage equation studies. These studies show direct evidence of discrimination.

On balance, the evidence indicates that sex discrimination remains a possible explanation of the unexplained gender pay gap. This is consistent with the continuing high-profile sex discrimination litigation suggestive of ongoing inferior treatment on the basis of sex.

2

Background on Labor Force Participation, Earnings, and Occupation

This section provides statistics on trends in the labor market. The most visible outcomes of market work are labor force participation, earnings, and occupation. As the tables provided here demonstrate, female/male differences have lessened over time, although a substantial gap in pay remains.

Table 2.1 provides evidence on labor force participation in selected years over the period 1970–2004. Perhaps the most notable change in the labor market over the past 35 years is the dramatic increase in the female labor force participation rate, with the less dramatic but steady decline in the male labor force participation rate. In 1970, women were only slightly more than half as likely as men to be employed or seeking employment. By 2004, the labor force participation rate of women was 81 percent of men's. Women now comprise over 46 percent of the total employed workforce.

Table 2.2 reports median weekly earnings of female and male full-time wage and salary workers in selected years. In 1979, the ratio of female to male earnings was 62.3 percent. By 2004, a mere 25 years later, women's earnings are 80 percent of men's.

Table 2.1 Labor force participation rates, selected years 1970–2004.

	1970	1980	1990	2000	2004
Female	43.3	51.5	57.5	59.9	59.2
Male	79.7	77.4	76.4	74.8	73.3
F/M %	54.3	66.5	75.3	80.1	80.8

Note: Noninstitutional population age 16 years and over, annual averages.
Source: U.S. Department of Labor, *Women in the Labor Force: A Databook* (2005). Adapted from Table 2.

Table 2.2 Median usual weekly earnings of full-time wage and salary workers in current dollars, selected years 1979–2004.

	1979	1980	1990	2000	2004
Female	182	201	346	493	573
Male	292	313	481	641	713
F/M %	62.3	64.2	71.9	76.9	80.4

Source: U.S. Department of Labor, *Women in the Labor Force: A Databook* (2005). Adapted from Table 16.

In part, wage disparities arise from differences in occupation. Table 2.3 provides an overview of trends in occupation by gender based on broad occupational categories. In 1983, women comprised nearly 44 percent of total employment. The female share of total employment rose slightly to nearly 47 percent by 2002. There are clear differences in broad occupation, with women underrepresented in blue-collar jobs. The largest increase in female share of occupational employment between 1983 and 2002 occurred in managerial and professional specialty occupations. By 2002, slightly over half of those employed in managerial and professional specialty occupations were women, up from 41 percent in 1983. The female share of employment in technical, sales, administrative support, and service occupations remained fairly steady, with female employees comprising 60 percent or more of the workers in these occupations.

While the influx of women into managerial and professional specialty occupations would seem to contribute to the narrowing of the gender pay gap, examination of narrower occupation categories shows that women generally fare worse relative to men within these occupations. Based on full-time wage and salary workers in 2004, Table 2.4 reports employment, percent female, male median weekly earnings, and

Table 2.3 Percent female in major occupation, 1983 and 2002.

	1983		2002	
	Number in occupation (thousands)	Percent female	Number in occupation (thousands)	Percent female
Total, 16 years and over	100,834	43.7	136,485	46.6
Managerial and professional specialty	23,592	40.9	42,482	50.5
Technical, sales, and administrative support	31,265	64.6	38,947	63.4
Service occupations	13,857	60.1	19,219	59.9
Precision production, craft, and repair	12,328	8.1	14,660	8.2
Operators, fabricators, and laborers	16,091	26.6	17,697	22.7
Farming, forestry, and fishing	3,700	16.0	3,480	20.6

Note: The years 1983 and 2002 are used to compare occupations because occupational categories were revised in 2003. Due to the revision, these categories do not directly correspond to categories used to compare female to male earnings reported in Table 4.
Source: U.S. Department of Labor, Women in the Labor Force: A Databook (2005). Adapted from Table 10.

female median earnings as a percentage of male median earnings. Note the considerable variation in median pay among occupations. Managerial and professional occupations are generally the highest paying. But we also see that in many of the managerial and professional occupations, the female to male ratio is actually lower than the overall female to male earnings ratio of 80.4 percent. For example, among managers, women's earnings are 72 percent of men's. In none of these occupational groups do women's earnings exceed even 90 percent of men's earnings. Women's earnings are closest to men's in low-paying occupations, such as healthcare support, food preparation and serving related, office and administrative support, and farming, fishing, and forestry. Women employed in installation, maintenance, and repair occupations have earnings that are 86.4 percent of men's, but women comprise only 4.4 percent of employment in these occupations.[1]

[1] It is of interest to note that in 2004, female full-time wage and salary workers have higher median weekly earnings than men in seven narrowly defined (three-digit) occupations. These occupations and the ratio of female to male earnings are as follows: Food preparation workers, 101.3; dining room and cafeteria attendants and bartender helpers, 109.2; bill and account collectors, 101.9; reservation and transportation ticket agents and travel clerks,

Table 2.4 Occupational employment, median usual weekly earnings, and female to male earnings ratio, full-time wage and salary workers, 2004 annual averages (numbers in thousands).

	Total employed	Percent female in occupation	Male median weekly earnings	Female earnings as percent of men's
Total, 16 years and over	101,224	43.7	713	80.4
Management	10,221	39.1	1,215	71.7
Business and financial operations	4,558	57.3	1,007	74.1
Computer and mathematical	2,793	27.1	1,155	84.2
Architecture and engineering	2,500	13.2	1,139	77.3
Life, physical, and social science	1,073	39.7	1,012	87.4
Community and social services	1,848	58.6	766	86.3
Legal	1,111	54.3	1,561	54.1
Education, training, and library	5,941	71.9	956	76.3
Arts, design, entertainment, sports, and media	1,426	43.3	862	79.8
Healthcare practitioner and technical	4,680	74.1	1,062	76.1
Healthcare support	1,985	88.4	453	88.7
Protective service	2,509	18.8	733	76.0
Food preparation and serving related	3,863	49.4	384	88.3
Building and grounds cleaning and maintenance	3,436	35.2	412	81.3
Personal care and service	1,969	72.7	500	76.0
Sales and related	9,984	44.3	747	62.1
Office and administrative support	14,966	74.3	587	88.9
Farming, fishing, and forestry	718	18.5	367	87.7
Construction and extraction	6,232	2.0	606	83.2
Installation, maintenance, and repair	4,330	4.4	707	86.4
Production	8,478	28.9	597	67.8
Transportation and material moving	6,604	12.7	549	74.7

Source: U.S. Department of Labor, *Women in the Labor Force: A Databook* (2005). Adapted from Table 18.

Table 2.4 also demonstrates how broad occupational categories mask considerable sorting by sex within broad occupational category. Although about half of those employed in managerial and professional specialty occupations are female, only 27 percent of those employed in computer and mathematical occupations are female, as are only 13 percent of those in architecture and engineering occupations. But 57 percent of those employed in business and financial operations occupations are female, as are 72 percent of those in education, training, and library occupations, 88 percent of those employed in healthcare support, and 74 percent of those in office and administrative support occupations.

102.0; postal service clerks, 102.2; computer operators, 100.9; mail clerks and mail machine operators except postal service, 110.6. These seven occupations employ 1.9 percent of the total employment of full-time wage and salary workers and therefore have little impact on the overall female to male ratio.

3

Measuring Pay Disparities

Pay disparities can arise from differences in work-related characteristics as well as from differential treatment by the market of these characteristics. Earnings differences due to differences in average characteristics are referred to as "explained," and differences in returns to characteristics are "unexplained." The portion unexplained by individual characteristics is frequently interpreted as a measure of discrimination.

3.1 Oaxaca–Blinder Decomposition Method

To estimate the amount of any pay disparity due to differences in returns to levels of characteristics as well as due to different returns to characteristics, the decomposition method of Oaxaca (1973) and Blinder (1973) is widely used. Their decomposition procedure is performed by estimating log wage equations separately for male and female workers. The log wage equations for men and women can be written as

$$\ln w_{\mathrm{m}} = X_{\mathrm{m}} b_{\mathrm{m}}, \tag{3.1}$$

$$\ln w_{\mathrm{f}} = X_{\mathrm{f}} b_{\mathrm{f}}, \tag{3.2}$$

where $\ln w_{\mathrm{m}}$ and $\ln w_{\mathrm{f}}$ are the average log wages for men and women, respectively, X_{m} and X_{f} are vectors of average values of the explanatory variables, and $b_{\rm m}$ and $b_{\rm f}$ are the vectors of estimated coefficients from the log wage Eqs. (3.1) and (3.2).

Subtracting (3.2) from (3.1) yields

$$\ln w_{\rm m} - \ln w_{\rm f} = X_{\rm m}b_{\rm m} - X_{\rm f}b_{\rm f}. \tag{3.3}$$

We can now rearrange Eq. (3.3) in two equivalent ways. By adding and subtracting to Eq. (3.3) the term $X_{\rm f}b_{\rm m}$, and grouping the terms, we can rewrite Eq. (3.3) as

$$\ln w_{\rm m} - \ln w_{\rm f} = (X_{\rm m} - X_{\rm f})b_{\rm m} + X_{\rm f}(b_{\rm m} - b_{\rm f}). \tag{3.4}$$

By adding and subtracting $X_{\rm m}b_{\rm f}$ to Eq. (3.3), the log wage gap can alternatively be written as

$$\ln w_{\rm m} - \ln w_{\rm f} = (X_{\rm m} - X_{\rm f})b_{\rm f} + X_{\rm m}(b_{\rm m} - b_{\rm f}). \tag{3.5}$$

Equations (3.4) and (3.5) decompose the total log wage gap $\ln w_{\rm m} - \ln w_{\rm f}$ into two parts. The first term on the right-hand side of Eqs. (3.4) and (3.5) represents the component of the log wage gap arising from gender difference in average characteristics $(X_{\rm m} - X_{\rm f})$ where differences in these characteristics are "valued" using the male regression coefficients in Eq. (3.4) and using the female coefficients in Eq. (3.5). The second term on the right-hand side in each equation is the portion of the log wage gap due to differences in the wage structure faced by males and females. This component is not explained by differences in average characteristics and is thereby frequently interpreted as a measure of discrimination.

It is clear that the decompositions differ only in the choice of weights on the disparities $(X_{\rm m} - X_{\rm f})$ and $(b_{\rm m} - b_{\rm f})$. Equation (3.4) assumes that the male wage structure is the nondiscriminatory structure, while Eq. (3.5) assumes that the female wage structure is the nondiscriminatory structure. The values can differ considerably based on which wage structure is assumed to be the nondiscriminatory structure.

Of course, neither the current wage structure faced by females or by males may be the structure that would be observed in the absence of discrimination. A generalized decomposition that includes both (3.4) and (3.5) as special cases is

$$\ln w_{\rm m} - \ln w_{\rm f} = (X_{\rm m} - X_{\rm f})b + [X_{\rm m}(b_{\rm m} - b) - X_{\rm f}(b_{\rm f} - b)], \tag{3.6}$$

where b is the coefficients in the no-discrimination wage structure (Neumark, 1988). If in the absence of discrimination the male wage structure would prevail, $b = b_m$, and Eq. (3.6) reduces to Eq. (3.4). Similarly, if in the absence of discrimination the female wage structure would prevail, Eq. (3.6) reduces to Eq. (3.5). The actual form of the no-discrimination wage structure depends on the form of employers' discriminatory behavior. One plausible possibility is suggested by Neumark (1988), who shows that if employers care only about the relative proportion of male and female workers, then the no-discrimination structure is represented by the coefficients derived from regressions pooling males and females.

For any given raw wage gap, typically less than half of the wage gap is explained by differences in characteristics. For example, using Current Population Survey (CPS) data for 1979 and 1995 and controlling for education, experience, personal characteristics, city and region, occupation, industry, government employment, and part-time status, Altonji and Blank (1999) find that only about 27 percent of the gender wage gap in each year is explained by differences in characteristics. Also using CPS data, Boraas and Rodgers (2003) estimate a similar specification augmented by percent female in occupation. They report that only 39 percent of the gender pay gap is explained in 1999, controlling for percent female, schooling, potential experience, region, SMSA size, minority status, part-time employment, marital status, union, government employment, and industry. The explained share is somewhat higher in 1989 and 1992 based on the same specification, with the explained share 58 percent in 1989 and 53 percent in 1992.

Because these decompositions and measures of discrimination are widely reported, it is worthwhile to keep in mind some of the limitations. A key criticism is that productivity measures are only partially accounted for, so any unexplained disparity can always be attributed to something not included in the regression. If men fare better on the omitted characteristics, then the pay gap is overstated. Related to this point is the accuracy of measured human capital. In particular, men average more years of labor market experience. Because data on actual labor market experience is not available in some of the larger, widely used data sets, such as the CPS, potential experience, equal to age minus years of education minus 5, is used as a proxy for actual experience. This then overstates actual labor market experience for women. Finding differences in the returns to experience does not necessarily say anything about discrimination but may instead be reflective of different location by gender on the actual wage–experience profile. A related point is that the same level of measured characteristics may represent different amounts of human capital for men and women. In earlier periods, women's expectations to drop out of the labor force for family reasons would result in lower actual investment in human capital, even for men and women with the same measured years of education or experience (Polachek, 1975a, Sandell and Shapiro, 1980). If so, the return to human capital characteristics could differ by gender for nondiscriminatory reasons.[1]

Although differences in characteristics are considered to be part of the explained nondiscriminatory share of the wage gap, these characteristics may be influenced by discrimination. The presence and magnitude of discrimination therefore may be understated, as the control variables themselves are influenced by discrimination.

There are also a number of modeling decisions that underlie the wage regressions, and the estimates of discrimination tend to be influenced by specification. While hourly wage is preferred, it is not always available, and regressions using annual salary or weekly salary conflate labor supply with earnings. It was the norm for a number of years following Heckman (1979) to correct for selection into the labor force for women. However, identifying the wage equation is almost always problematic, as it is unusual to have valid instruments that explain labor force participation but do not themselves influence wages.[2] Misspecification can generate large biases in estimates (Manski, 1989). Ashraf

[1] While the human capital literature stresses that women's expectations to drop out of the labor market lead to lesser market investments and a lower return to these investments, Hersch and Reagan (1997) show that if men and women differ only in their expected time in the labor market, efficient wage–tenure profiles are steeper for women than men to induce optimal effort. A number of empirical studies, reviewed in Hersch and Reagan, find a steeper wage–tenure profile for women.

[2] Technically the wage equation is identified by functional form but such results are less persuasive as they do not derive from a theoretical basis.

(1996) finds that the selectivity coefficient was significant in only 1 of 16 regressions estimated for separate years, suggesting that selection is random after controlling for observables. Whether to control for occupation, industry, job training, college major, and so forth, is debatable, as such outcomes themselves are almost certainly influenced by (actual or potential) discrimination. Studies with extensive controls for characteristics highly correlated with gender unsurprisingly greatly reduce or eliminate the wage gap. The construction of the sample likewise strongly influences whether a discriminatory gap is measured, with the smallest gaps (or no gap) measured among new entrants (as for lawyers in Hersch, 2003) or those not married (Fishback and Terza, 1989).

A recent example that demonstrates the interpretation problem inherent in the decomposition approach to measuring discrimination is by O'Neill and O'Neill (2005). O'Neill and O'Neill use data from the National Longitudinal Survey of Youth 1979 (NLSY79). The NLSY79 is a nationally representative survey of young men and women who were born during 1957–1964, and are 14–22 years old when first interviewed in 1979. O'Neill and O'Neill's analysis leaves a considerable unexplained gap even controlling for AFQT, education, and actual work history, including proportion of work time that was part time, indicators for whether first birth was before age 30 years or at least age 30 years, and whether the women ever had a spell outside of the labor force due to family responsibilities, as well as for percent female in the occupation, measures of occupational characteristics derived from the Dictionary of Occupational Titles (DOT) and computer use derived from CPS supplements.

Despite unusually extensive and seemingly comprehensive controls for choice, O'Neill and O'Neill conclude that the unexplained gap is due to difference in choices about amount of time and energy devoted to a career, as indicated by the greater proportion of women who had part-time work and were employed in the nonprofit sector (even though the gap remains when these controls are included). They draw this conclusion in part from the regression restricted to childless, never-married men and women, which shows that women have a higher wage without adjustments, but that advantage disappears with controls and turns into an insignificant disadvantage of 2.7 percent.[3] They conclude by noting, "Our analysis indicates that women choose occupations and job settings that are compatible with combining market and home work. It would be difficult to find an explanation based on employer choice that could explain the observed patterns."

What O'Neill and O'Neill's interpretation of their findings implies is that no matter how comprehensive is the regression model, or how large of an unexplained component remains, it is always possible to claim that unobserved differences in choices are actually driving unexplained pay disparities. Most researchers, however, find the existence of wage gaps that are not explained by gender differences in characteristics as evidence in support of possible discrimination.

3.2 Wage Inequality and the Gender Pay Disparity

Wage inequality increased during the 1980s. Juhn *et al.* (1991, 1993), advance the argument that this rising wage inequality is due to an increase in the return to skills. They provide a decomposition that adds two new components to the Oaxaca–Blinder decomposition. Their approach compares changes for a cohort over time to changes of cohorts of the same age. Workers are assigned a percentile rank in the residual wage distribution. Changes in the residual difference between two groups are then decomposed into changes in the differences in their mean percentile ranks, which is interpreted as changes in the level of unmeasured skill, and changes in the dispersion of the residual wage distribution, which is interpreted as changes in the returns to skill.[4]

Blau and Kahn (1997) employ this decomposition method to explain the seeming paradox of widening wage inequality and a narrowing gender gap over the same period in the 1980s. The nature of the paradox is

[3] As we will see in our discussion of the influence of family status on earnings, the seeming gender parity among never-married men and women derives from the very low pay for never-married men, and the fact that most such individuals are at an early age and stage of their work lives.

[4] The importance of growing residual wage inequality in explaining most of the growth in wage inequality is called into question by Lemieux (2006), who shows that the role of residual wage inequality is considerably diminished when controlling for changing composition of the workforce and using data with a better measure of hourly wage.

that women who have lower average observable labor market skills (e.g., work experience) and are located disproportionately in lower-paying occupations and industries should have been made worse off by a wage structure that increases the price of skills in higher skilled sectors. Blau and Kahn's analysis finds that but for the rising inequality and higher rewards to skills, women would have made more progress in narrowing the wage gap. Their estimates indicate that the gap would have been 5–6 percentage points lower if the wage structure had remained stable. But the gap declined because women's relative qualifications improved (particularly with respect to experience and occupation) as well as due to a narrowing of the unexplained component of the pay structure. This narrowing may have happened because women also improved their relative level of unmeasured characteristics.[5]

Fortin and Lemieux (1998) also find that women's increased labor market experience contributed to the narrowing of the gap, performing a decomposition at each percentile of the wage distribution, as well as considering that the changes in the relative position of women will affect the overall wage distribution (in contrast to Blau and Kahn who assume that the male wage distribution will be unaffected by changes in the relative position of women).

The residual gender wage gap can also be used to test theories of discrimination. Theory implies that wage gaps should be smallest in more competitive environments. Black and Brainerd (2004) examine the impact of increased competition from trade in competitive and concentrated industries. The wage gap in industries that are already competitive should experience little decrease in the wage gap as trade increases, while wage gaps in concentrated industries should narrow in response to competitive pressures. Black and Brainerd use the import share at the three-digit industry level as a measure of competition from trade and classify an industry as concentrated if the four-firm concentration ratio was 0.40 or greater in 1977. The dependent variable is calculated by first regressing log wage on education, age, and nonwhite using individual data from the March CPS over the periods 1977–1994,

[5] Note, however, that Suen (1997) demonstrates within a theoretical framework that this interpretation is valid only if there is no discrimination.

as well as from the CPS Outgoing Rotation Groups and the 1980 and 1990 Censuses. The change in the average residual gender wage gap at the industry or MSA level is then regressed on whether an industry is concentrated, import share, and the interaction of concentration with import share. The findings indicate that increased competition from trade reduces the residual wage gap in concentrated industries, thus supporting the theory and indicating discrimination that may erode over time in response to competitive pressures.

4

Occupational Segregation

There are long-standing disparities by gender in occupational distribution. Although there is more similarity now, as shown in Table 2.4, many occupations disproportionately employ mainly men or women. Women still comprise the vast majority of those employed as nurses, pre-college teachers, social workers, and office and administrative support workers. Most engineers and construction workers are male. Substantial evidence shows an inverse relation between the proportion of females in an occupation and wages for both men and women (e.g., Macpherson and Hirsch, 1995, Boraas and Rodgers, 2003). The importance of sex segregation in contributing to the gender pay gap cannot be overstated. Groshen (1991) shows that most of the pay gap is explained by sex segregation within occupations, industries, and establishments rather than by wage differences.

Occupational segregation is predicted from several theories. In Becker's (1957) model of taste discrimination, at the extreme, discriminatory tastes of employers, coworkers, or customers result in firms segregated by sex.[1] Bergmann's (1974) model of occupational crowding

[1] Neumark (1988) modifies the Becker model to allow employers to care about the relative share of females to males, thus resulting in less than complete segregation.

shows how segregation can lower women's earnings by shifting to the right the labor supply curve of women within the few occupations open to women, thereby depressing wages within these occupations. Explanations of occupational segregation based on individual choice imply that women anticipating weaker labor force attachment will choose occupations in which the cost of intermittency is lower (Mincer and Polachek, 1974).[2] Breen and García-Peñalosa (2002) model gender segregation arising in a Bayesian learning framework as prior beliefs about the probability of success are transmitted from mother to daughter and father to son. Preferences of earlier generations over gender roles will influence current segregation. Statistical discrimination can in some cases lead to segregation as employers make hiring decisions based on predicted productivity of the group (Phelps, 1972, Arrow, 1973).

In this section, I discuss how occupational segregation is measured and provide an overview of studies that examine the impact of occupational segregation on the gender pay gap.

4.1 Measuring Segregation

Occupational segregation is usually summarized by the index of dissimilarity, also called the "segregation index." This is calculated as

$$D = \frac{1}{2}\sum_{i=1}^{I} |p_{\mathrm{im}} - p_{\mathrm{if}}|,$$

where p_{im} and p_{if} represent the proportion of males (females) in the labor force employed in occupation i, and I is the number of occupational categories. If women and men are proportionately represented in every occupation, the index will have the value of zero. Complete

[2] Polachek (1981) demonstrates that women choose occupations with lower rates of atrophy, where atrophy is measured as the coefficient on home time in a wage regression. Thus occupational segregation arises from human capital optimizing behavior. England (1982) points out that both wage appreciation and depreciation will affect occupational choice and shows that wage growth is not affected by the gender composition of occupations, nor is gender composition of first jobs correlated with eventual time in the labor market. By examining the timing of labor market intermittency, Robst and VanGilder (2000) show that gender composition of occupations does affect depreciation rates for married women, with depreciation rates lower for married women in female occupations than in male occupations.

segregation would result in an index value of 100. D represents the proportion of women who would have to change occupations to achieve an equal proportion of men and women across all occupations. The value of the index depends on the detail of occupation classifications. Based on the Census three-digit detailed occupations, the segregation index was around 65 for much of the 20th century but dropped to around 50 over the period 1970–1990 (Reskin and Bielby, 2005). Macpherson and Hirsch (1995) report a measure of D based on three-digit occupations that declined steadily from 68.5 in 1973–1974 to 54.6 in 1993.

Note that D (as well as other indices) has shortcomings as a measure of segregation. It is not invariant to the units of measurement of occupation. Calculations using three-digit occupation codes indicate greater segregation than calculations based on two-digit codes. These indices are influenced by changes in labor force participation and by trends in the economy, such as the movement from manufacturing to services. The measures also depend on the fineness with which occupations are reported. Historically blue-collar occupations held primarily by men have been divided into narrower categories than have administrative support positions held primarily by women. Nonetheless such measures are valuable in examining trends over time.

4.2 The Influence of Segregation on the Gender Pay Disparity

There are two main approaches to examining the effect of segregation on earnings. The most common approach is to estimate a conventional wage equation adding a control for percent female in occupation. Because such aggregate statistics may mask substantial segregation at the level of the firm or jobs within firms, the second approach looks at sorting by sex into different employers, and within employers, into different narrowly defined jobs. The data demands of the latter approach are far more extensive, and such studies are rarer (see e.g., Blau, 1977, Groshen, 1991, Bayard *et al.*, 2003). Regardless of the level of detail of the data, an unexplained gender gap remains even with controls for segregation.

Wage equations controlling for percent female in occupation invariably find a negative coefficient on percent female for both men and women. One interpretation is that women face barriers to higher-paying occupations, and that men who do not face such barriers but end up in lower-paying female occupations are of inferior quality. Alternatively, in the absence of gender discrimination, preferences for working conditions that warrant a compensating wage differential can also explain why female occupations have lower pay.[3]

To explore these issues, Macpherson and Hirsch (1995) use information on gender composition and wages from the CPS over a 20-year period (1973–1993) matched with data on occupational characteristics and working conditions from various CPS supplements as well as the DOT. Macpherson and Hirsch's standard wage equation specification controls for education, potential experience, race, marital status, full-time employment, public sector employment, metropolitan area, region, industry, and occupation. The additional job characteristics in their expanded wage equations include measures calculated from CPS supplements of occupational tenure, part-time employment share, on-the-job training, and computer use, as well as measures from the DOT of training requirements, strength, hazards, and physical and environmental working conditions. By using the panel nature of the CPS data, Macpherson and Hirsch are able to net out individual fixed effects, and by controlling for detailed job characteristics, they control in part for working conditions. They find that the coefficient on percent female is about half the size in their differences specification than in levels, and that controlling for job characteristics lowers the effect of percent female to about one-third to two-thirds the original size relative to the standard estimates in either levels or changes. They conclude that two-thirds of the originally observed negative gender composition effect is due to unmeasured person-specific quality or preferences and measured differences in job skills and characteristics.

Macpherson and Hirsch also examine how inclusion of percent female in the occupation affects the explained and unexplained

[3] The stratification perspective of sociology would interpret the negative relation between earnings and proportion female as resulting from cultural devaluation of predominantly female activities.

components of the gender wage gap over time. It is noteworthy that even with these extensive controls and inclusion of percent female, much less than half of the gender wage gap is explained by observable characteristics. For example, of the total log wage gap of 0.235 (26 percent) in 1993, only 0.090, or 38 percent of the total wage gap, is explained by these extensive control variables. Gender composition explains a relatively minor share of the gap, as do the additional job characteristics. What we can infer from these results is that occupational crowding is not likely to be an important explanation of the gender pay gap.

5

Turnover

Expected differences by gender in turnover are fundamental to most explanations of the gender pay disparity. Choice-based explanations stress the optimality of different investments and occupations arising from gender differences in labor market commitment. Models based on statistical discrimination require that labor market characteristics of women are less predictable than those of men. While women tend to have less total experience, there is less evidence that women have lower within-employer tenure than do men. Although women quit more often for family-related reasons, men quit more often to move to another job. Furthermore, men have higher layoff rates (Blau and Kahn, 1981, Keith and McWilliams, 1995).

5.1 Background Data

Table 5.1 reports statistics on median years of tenure over the period 1983–2004 from various CPS supplements on tenure. Employees are asked how long they had worked continuously for their current

Table 5.1 Median years of tenure with current employer for employed wage and salary workers age 25 years and over, selected years.

	January 1983	January 1991	February 1998	January 2004
Female	4.2	4.3	4.4	4.7
Male	5.9	5.4	4.9	5.1
F/M %	71.2	79.6	89.8	92.2

Source: U.S. Department of Labor, *Employee Tenure in 2004*. Adapted from Table 1, available at www.bls.gov/news.release/pdf/tenure.pdf.

Table 5.2 Number of jobs held and percent of total weeks not in the labor force from age 18 to 38 years in 1978–2002.

	Average number of jobs	Percent of total weeks not in the labor force
Female	9.9	26.3
Male	10.4	10.5
F/M %	95.2	250.5

Source: *National Longitudinal Survey of Youth 1979*. Adapted from report at http://www.bls.gov/news.release/pdf/nlsoy.pdf, Tables 1 and 3.

employer.[1] Table 5.1 shows that gender differences in tenure have not been that dramatic, at least by 1983, and that only a small difference remains to this date.

Table 5.2 reports statistics on number of jobs held and weeks not worked calculated from the NLSY79. These statistics are based on the sample of 7,724 individuals who responded to the 2002 wave of the NLSY79 and are calculated using the period of their lives in which they were age 18–38 years. Jobs are defined as an uninterrupted period of work with a particular employer. For self-employed workers, each new job is defined by the individual. Men average slightly more jobs over this period, with both men and women averaging about 10 jobs in this 20-year span at the beginning of their work histories. Women spend slightly more than a quarter of their time not in the labor force, while men spend only 10.5 percent of their time not in the labor force.

There are two lines of research related to turnover. First, does turnover differ by gender, controlling for job characteristics? Second, does turnover affect wages, and by what mechanism? Theory alone

[1] Earlier years of tenure data are not reported because the CPS question did not distinguish whether individuals reported tenure on the job or tenure with the employer.

does not yield clear predictions on whether men or women would have higher quit rates. Search models assume that individuals maximize their expected discounted lifetime income net of search costs. The decision to quit to either unemployment or for a better job depends on the expected wage offer distribution, search costs, and the opportunity cost (equal to current wage rate). For instance, if men have longer expected total duration in the labor market, the gains from search and mobility will be higher for men, increasing their quit rate. A related point is that if women are constrained in their job search, for instance due to restricted mobility for family reasons, then at the same wage rate women would have lower quit rates than men.

The second question is how turnover affects wages. There are two main mechanisms with contradictory predictions. One mechanism is the effect of turnover on on-the-job training. In this framework, higher (actual or expected) turnover would lead to lower investment in on-the-job training and lower wage growth. In contrast, search models indicate that turnover results in better paying jobs and match quality. Since mobility is associated with higher wage rates, men's greater job-to-job mobility may lead to higher wages than does women's job-to-nonemployment mobility. In a simple search model, gains from additional search depend on expected job duration. If men expect longer duration on any job, then they will have a higher reservation wage. Search costs may be higher for women who have less experience in the labor market or who are responsible for childcare.

Table 5.3 summarizes some of the factors that affect voluntary and involuntary turnover, with predictions of whether men or women will have higher rates for the specified reasons.

5.2 Does Turnover Differ by Gender?

There are alternative empirical approaches used to test for gender disparities in turnover. Some studies use probit to test whether the individual quits his or her job during that period, or alternatively, multinomial probit to allow for different destinations (employment, unemployment, not in labor force). Other studies use proportional hazard models to estimate parameters of models of duration to exit. Hazard

Table 5.3 Predicted turnover differences by gender.

Reason	Explanation	Predicted higher turnover rate for
Family	Bearing and raising children	Women
Family migration decisions	Wives may quit jobs if higher paid husbands move or wives may face geographic limits restricting job mobility	Uncertain
Matching and information	Ability to learn match quality may depend on total labor market experience, hence, women with less labor market experience may make inferior matches	Women
Search	Greater expected duration in labor market, greater gains to search	Men
Discrimination	Coworker discrimination may increase quits but limited outside opportunities due to discrimination will reduce quits	Uncertain
Layoffs	Cyclical industries will have higher layoffs	Men
Specific investment	Greater specific investment, fewer alternative jobs will pay more	Women
Search costs	May be higher for women if search inefficient for women due to lower labor market experience and due to high opportunity cost of time in household responsibilities	Men
Secondary earner	Women may enter and exit labor force over business cycles	Women

models can be estimated in discrete time or in continuous time. In part this depends on the frequency of data. Proportional hazard models require distributional assumptions, or the Box-Cox model can be used to estimate the functional form implied by the data. Censoring at both ends is likely to be present, and some studies resolve the left censoring issue by examining workers in their first jobs using, say, the NLSY79. The usual question of whether to control for occupation and industry arises in the modeling decision. Most studies control for wage, but not all. Inclusion of wage serves as a proxy for investment in specific capital and is expected to have a negative effect on quit rates as alternative wage offers are less likely to be higher. The results, however, are not generally driven by whether or not wage is included as a control variable.

Before individual panel data became available, studies that examine gender differences in quits use aggregate data. An early study is by Barnes and Jones (1974). This study uses as the dependent variable the average quit rate over the period 1950–1968 for females and for males in 19 two-digit industries, controlling for the proportion of young and old workers of each sex in the industry as well as controlling for average industry wage by sex. Higher wages are associated with lower industry quit rates for both men and women, with the coefficient on female quit rates three times that of males.[2]

Individual panel data provides a better method for analyzing quit rates as it allows controlling for individual-specific and job characteristics, and most studies of gender differences in quits are based on individual panel data. Two widely used datasets are the Panel Study to Income Dynamics (PSID) and various waves of the National Longitudinal Survey (NLS). These datasets contain extensive information on individual characteristics, and most or all of the studies discussed here control for demographic information including race, education, number of children, marital status, age (or alternatively work experience), and health status. Studies vary in whether controls for union status, industry, occupation, or percent female in industry or occupation are included. Studies also vary in whether controls for general labor market conditions, such as local unemployment rates, are included. Controls for metropolitan status and region are also generally included as they reflect labor market opportunities.

Because of known properties of duration dependence with respect to tenure, studies in this area control for tenure, in some cases distinguishing between low tenure of less than one year and more than one year of tenure. Turnover is highest in the first year of a job. Studies also differ in whether and how they control for wage. The inclusion of wage in quit equations can be interpreted as a proxy for human capital characteristics that influence the wage rate, which in turn influences the quit decision. Some studies (e.g., Viscusi, 1980) also control for the difference between actual and predicted wage, which tests whether workers who earn more than predicted are less likely to quit.

The two key early studies in this area are by Viscusi (1980) and Blau and Kahn (1981). Both studies demonstrate that women actually have

[2] Sample mean of quit rates and wages were not reported, but my rough calculations yield elasticities of −0.91 for women and −0.67 for men assuming average wages equal to national values at the time period.

lower quit rates than men controlling for job characteristics. Viscusi (1980) uses data from the 1975 and 1976 PSID to examine whether the individual had quit the job held in 1975 by 1976. Overall the unadjusted female quit rate was double the male quit rates (0.084 and 0.167). Breaking down quit rates by tenure shows that quit rates are highest in the first year of tenure, with quit rates of 13.6 and 28.0 for males and females. But males and females with more than one year of tenure have similar unadjusted quit rates, with male quit rates higher or lower than females depending on tenure (indeed, the quit rate for men with 1–2 years of tenure is nearly double that of corresponding women, 10.5 to 5.4). However, females are more likely than men to have less than one year of tenure, with nearly half the women in the sample having less than one year of tenure, in contrast to a little more than one-quarter of the males.

Logit estimates reveal the source of the gender disparity. The equations control for wage or difference between actual and predicted wage as well as demographic information (age, race, education, number of children, married, and health status), tenure, tenure less than one year, union, region, industry injury and illness rate, industry percent female, and area unemployment rate. Controlling for injury rates is atypical in such studies. If workers are not informed about injury risk, or are not compensated for such risk, quit probability may increase, and this may vary by gender. Preliminary tests show that quit equations need to be estimated separately for men and women. The key factor leading to higher female quit rates is that the female coefficient on less than one year of tenure is over two times the size of the coefficient for men, in combination with the fact that women are far more likely than men to have less than one year of tenure. After one year, tenure has no effect on quit rates. Viscusi finds similar elasticities of quits with respect to wage of −0.93 for both sexes, and likewise similar elasticities with respect to the wage gap (−0.42 for males and −0.48 for females). This indicates that the quit propensities of men and women with respect to wage do not differ.

Viscusi's finding of similar elasticities of quits with respect to wage for men and women is relevant to understanding the gender pay gap. Workers who are less responsive to financial incentives would be paid less, all else equal. But because men and women have similar elasticities of quits with respect to wage, this cannot explain women's lower wages. These logit regression results indicate that unadjusted sex differences in quit rates are due to differences in job characteristics rather than behavior or personal characteristics. In fact, substituting female values of explanatory variables into the male equations shows that the female quit rate would increase if females faced the male quit equation. Similarly, if women had the same characteristics as men, and continued to face the female equation, their quit rate would be below men's.

Blau and Kahn (1981) perform an analysis of gender differences in quits using data from the NLS Young Men (NLSYM) and Young Women (NLSYW), using the years 1969–1970 and 1970–1971 for men; and 1970–1971 and 1971–1972 for women. Their dependent variable is whether the individual had voluntarily quit the initial job by the subsequent year's survey. They estimate separate probit equations for men and women by race. In contrast to Viscusi, which is based on workers of a wide age range, the individuals in these NLS surveys are considerably younger, as male sample members are 14–24 years in 1966, and female sample members are 14–24 years in 1968. But since most turnover occurs among the young, this is the age range which provides much of the observed turnover and captures turnover that occurs in the formative state of careers. The quit equations control for education, potential experience and its square, tenure, military service, or draft status if male, married, dependents, other family income, family assets, own hourly wage, log of median income of respondents sex in three-digit occupation, union, white-collar occupation, mining, construction or manufacturing industry, SMSA unemployment rate, south, and size of labor market.

Blau and Kahn find that those with greater tenure are less likely to quit, with the magnitude of the effect among both whites and blacks more than twice as large for males than for females. Blau and Kahn predict quit rates by substituting the average values of the male (female) characteristics into the female (male) equation. They find that women would be less likely than men to quit if women faced the male quit equation or if men faced the male equation but had the average characteristics of women. Furthermore, if instead of swapping all characteristics, consider just giving females the average male job characteristics (wage, income, collective bargaining, occupation, and industry). Again, the female quit rate would be below the male rate if females had male job characteristics.

These two papers, Viscusi (1980) and Blau and Kahn (1981), demonstrate that the apparent higher female quit rates are actually due to the worse jobs in which women are employed. If women had the job characteristics of men, their quit rate would be lower than that of men. This sheds light on statistical discrimination explanations of the gender wage gap. If employers believe that women have higher quit rates than men, they will use this information to statistically discriminate and refrain from hiring women in jobs with considerable training or fixed employment costs. Yet, this perception is invalid. However, statistical discrimination can arise even if mean quit rates are identical if the probability of quitting is more variable for one group due to risk aversion on the part of employers.

To follow up on the question as to whether greater variability among women in quit probability could support statistical discrimination, Light and Ureta (1992) examine whether employers indeed err more in predicting quits for women than for men. This paper uses the data set employed by Blau and Kahn (1981), the NLSYM and NLSYW, but over a longer period, specifically over the period 1966–1981 (men) and 1968–1985 (women), using the period when individuals were age 24–31 years. They analyze the sample as two cohorts, an early cohort (women born in 1944–1946 and men born in 1942–1944), and a late cohort (women born in 1952–1954 and men born 1950–1952). Light and Ureta estimate proportional hazard models with time-varying covariates, controlling for unobserved heterogeneity. (Examination of whether heterogeneity is individual-specific or job-match specific indicates that it is individual-specific.) Estimation uses a discrete time model to allow for the presence of time-varying regressors, with intervals of 3 months.

Light and Ureta start by estimating hazard equations controlling only for characteristics that can be observed at the time of hire. The next stage adds child and marriage characteristics that may influence turnover. The fullest specification controls for race, changes in marital status, whether a child is born, whether a child is age 6 years or younger, education, years of potential prior experience, ratio of actual to potential prior experience, gap in time between end of last job and start of new job, whether last job terminated involuntarily, whether initial occupation on new job is the same as last job, part-time, wage, union, industry, occupation, local unemployment rate, south, whether SMSA, and year indicators. The hazard estimates are then used to predict the probability that workers of different characteristics will have a job separation within the next 6 months.

Over the full age range, Light and Ureta find more unobserved heterogeneity among female workers. This implies that employers are less able to identify which women will quit than which men. However, stratification into the early and late cohorts reveals that within the more recent cohort, female quitters can be predicted more accurately than male quitters. Of the characteristics that may be unknown at hire, only the birth of a newborn has a substantial impact on female quits. That is, among more recent labor market participants, tenure can be predicted as accurately for female as male workers, particularly once fertility is completed.

Also of interest is whether the reasons for turnover differ by sex. Such information may help explain whether match quality or long- versus short-run factors differ by sex. Sicherman (1996) examines departures from a single firm (a large insurance company with headquarters in NYC and branches across the US) over the period 1971–1980 and examines reported information on the reason for departure. Controlling for personal characteristics, job grade, and tenure, he finds structural differences in the reported reason for quitting. Women report dissatisfaction with working conditions or a desire for "higher earnings" more frequently than do men, while men cite "greater opportunity" more frequently than do women. Sicherman interprets the findings to mean that men's mobility is explained by long-run career considerations while short-run market conditions are more important for women's mobility.

How gender differences in search affects turnover and whether discrimination plays a residual role is addressed by Bowlus (1997). Among the well-documented gender differences are the greater propensity of women to exit to nonemployment,[3] as well as the longer duration in nonemployment especially of those exiting to nonparticipation. Bowlus uses a search model of Mortensen (1990) allowing for three types of separation behavior rather than the two states used in Mortensen. The model sets up as competing hypotheses that the gender wage differential is generated by differences in behavior, or alternatively by differences in productivity. Discrimination is not explicitly modeled and, if present, would be reflected in the behavioral component and the productivity component. Specifically, any portion of the wage differential not explained by search patterns is attributed to productivity differences.

The search model used by Bowlus allows for transitions from unemployment to employment, job to job, and so forth, with transitions affected by the arrival rates of job offers in each state, the job destruction rate, and changes in the value of time in the nonparticipation state (which can be interpreted as changes in home production). The model is a conventional search model in which individuals adopt a reservation wage strategy. Exits to nonparticipation are exogenous. Gender differences in tendency to exit the labor market to nonparticipation would result in women having a lower reservation wage than men. If males and females operate in different markets (as would be consistent with observed sex segregation) then lower average wages for women would result in this framework by several means, such as a higher exit rate into nonparticipation that lowers the reservation wage.

Bowlus uses data from the NLSY79 for 1979–1991. The sample is restricted to white workers who are either high school graduates or those with 16 or more years of education. She finds that search accounts for 20–30 percent of the wage differential for high school graduates and 15–20 percent for college graduates, with on-the-job search accounting for even greater shares of the wage differential as on-the-job search moved workers up the wage offer distribution over time. The remainder is explained in this model as due to productivity differences.

---

[3] However, female high school graduates have longer first job durations than male high school graduates.

Royalty (1998) examines the roles of destination of turnover and level of education in explaining differences between men and women in turnover behavior. Using NLSY79 data for 1979–1987, the average stay probabilities of 68 percent for women and 67 percent for men do not differ significantly by gender. The role of education in influencing turnover varies with the destination of turnover. But women have lower average job-to-job turnover and higher job-to-nonemployment turnover than do men. Less educated women have higher job-to-nonemployment turnover, while more educated women have higher job-to-job turnover. Royalty estimates discrete multinomial probit equations controlling for tenure on current job and its square, actual labor market experience and its square, health status, union status, real wage on current job and its square, asset income, a married indicator variable, number of children, local unemployment rate, whether in school during the year, nonwhite indicator, and indicators for highest level of education. In sum, given the lack of difference between turnover, quit-type turnover does not explain the gender wage gap.

5.3 How Turnover Affects Wages

There is extensive literature documenting the negative wage effect of discontinuous labor force participation. There is also extensive literature documenting that voluntary job change results in higher wage growth than not changing or than involuntary change. But whether an individual exits to another job or leaves the labor force may have an effect on earnings at the next job that may differ by gender. Only expected tenure rather than destination after leaving will matter for employers concerned about fixed costs of hiring or sorting into jobs with lower training or capital. But, if job-to-job turnover represents improving match quality, then we would expect that wages will be higher for those whose turnover resulted in another job than for those who interrupt their job history with periods out of the labor force. Once the reason for job change is taken into account, there should be little gender difference in the return to mobility, which is what Keith and McWilliams (1997) find.

However, search behavior can differ by gender, and this may have an effect on wages. Search behavior of men and women may differ in intensity of search effort, reservation wage, or wage and offer functions. Intensity is inversely related to costs of search. While direct costs should not differ by gender, opportunity costs may be higher for women because the value of their time at home is higher. Reservation wages will be inversely related to search costs, suggesting that women's reservation wage will be lower than men's. The offer probability and wage offer functions may differ if search technology, such as use of informal versus formal means of search, differs by gender. Such gender differences can arise if women indeed have fewer informal or personal contacts due to occupational segregation or greater home time. Job mobility and search may interact, in that those who anticipate mobility can undertake search while still employed. Thus gender differences in returns to mobility can arise from different mobility patterns by gender, the likelihood of employed search may vary by mobility type or by gender, and there may be interactions between employed search and mobility.

Keith and McWilliams (1999) address gender differences in search behavior using NLSY79 data for 1979–1984. All job separations are classified as either a layoff, a discharge, a family-related quit, or a nonfamily-related quit. These years are used because information on employed job search is also available. Separations among these young workers are high, and although there are statistically significant gender differences in the likelihoods of separation, whether involuntary or not, and in the reason for separation, the magnitude of the differences are not stark. Most separations are quits, followed by layoffs, and only 8.4 percent of the female quits are for family-related reasons, compared to 3.8 percent of men's.

6

Children and Housework

Perhaps the most frequently offered reason for women's relative disadvantage in the labor market stems from the primary role women assume in the home. Only women bear children, and, regardless of marital status, women spend considerably more time than men on home production. Motherhood and household responsibilities may directly lower wages. Alternatively, lower pay for mothers and those with greater household responsibilities may arise because such women would be less productive even in the absence of childbirth and housework. Furthermore, these family choices may indirectly lower wages if women take jobs with work characteristics that warrant lower pay as a compensating differential for characteristics that are compatible with family and household responsibilities. Before discussing empirical studies, it is worthwhile to look at some statistics.

6.1 Children and Housework: Statistics

Often cited as the primary source of any gender disparity in economic outcomes is childbirth and childcare. Despite the arduous demands

Table 6.1 Labor force participation rates of females by age of youngest child, selected years 1975–2004.

	1975	1980	1990	2000	2004
No children under age 18 years	45.1	48.1	52.3	54.8	53.8
Youngest child under age 6 years	39.0	46.8	58.2	65.3	62.2
Youngest child age 6–17 years	54.9	64.3	74.7	79.0	77.5
Total	46.3	51.5	57.5	59.9	59.2

Notes: Noninstitutional population age 16 years and over, annual averages.
Source: U.S. Department of Labor, *Women in the Labor Force: A Databook* (2005). Adapted from Tables 2 and 7.

of motherhood, as shown in Table 6.1, it has long been common for mothers to participate in the labor force, even with children under age 6 years, and especially for those with children age 6 years and older. Since 1990, three-quarters or more of women whose youngest child is 6–17 years old have been in the labor force.

Table 6.2 suggests how the presence of children affects earnings of men and women. Note that regardless of marital status, women's earnings are highest among those without children under age 18 years. Men's earnings are the highest among those whose youngest child is ages 6–17 years. Not-married men and women have earnings considerably lower than their counterparts with the same children status, and the gender gap is narrower among not-married women and men. Notice the similarity of women and men's earnings among those not married and without children under age 18 years. The similarity of childless unmarried men and women is often cited as support for the premise that women's lower earnings derive from choices to exert less market effort because of marriage and children. It should be noted, however, that the similarity of earnings is mainly attributable to the low earnings of never-married men combined with most never-married and childless men and women being at an early point of their careers where there is little earnings disparity. Indeed, never-married men earn only 63.9 percent as much as married men.[1]

The U.S. Bureau of Labor Statistics (BLS) began collecting time use information in January 2003. This survey, the American Time

[1] Calculations from Table 1 of U.S. Department of Labor, *Highlights of Women's Earnings in 2004* (2005).

Table 6.2 Median usual weekly earnings of full-time wage and salary workers by sex, marital status, and presence and age of own children under 18 years old, 2004.

	Youngest child under 6 years	Youngest child 6–17 years	None under 18 years
Married, spouse present			
Female	592	591	615
Male	775	842	807
F/M %	76.4	70.2	76.2
Other marital statuses			
Female	423	519	546
Male	513	695	570
F/M %	82.4	74.7	95.8

Source: U.S. Department of Labor, *Highlights of Women's Earnings in 2004* (2005). Adapted from Table 8.

Use Survey (ATUS), is administered by means of a retrospective phone interview to a subsample of about 2000 individuals completing their final CPS interview. Diary responses to time use are grouped into broad categories, including market work time, leisure time, and personal care time. Of particular interest for our purposes is time spent on household activities and on childcare. Household activities include housework, food preparation and cleanup, lawn and garden care, and household management, as well as vehicle and home maintenance and repair, and pet care. Primary childcare includes physical care, playing with children, reading to children, assistance with homework, attending children's events, taking care of children's healthcare needs, and dropping off, picking up, and waiting for children. Other activities involving children, such as cooking for children, are included under household activities and not under childcare.

Tables 6.3 and 6.4 report statistics from the ATUS for 2004. Table 6.3 reports time per day spent on household activities and on childcare as the primary activity by sex, age of youngest child, and employment status. Table 6.4 reports time per day on household activities by sex and marital status. Time spent on household activities clearly depends on both sex and marital status, with women doing from 50 to 100 percent more than men, regardless of employment or marital status.

Table 6.3 Average hours per day spent on household activities and childcare by employment status and age of youngest household children, 2004.

	Household activities			Childcare	
	Age of youngest child			Age of youngest child	
	Under 6 years	6–17 years	None under 18 years	Under 6 years	6–17 years
Employed					
Female	2.03	2.01	1.74	2.19	0.69
Male	1.14	1.30	1.15	1.10	0.37
F/M	1.78	1.55	1.51	1.99	1.86
Not employed					
Female	3.29	3.38	2.92	2.87	1.10
Male	2.09	1.72	2.00	1.21	0.66
F/M	1.57	1.97	1.46	2.37	1.67

Source: U.S. Department of Labor, *American Time Use Survey, 2004*. Adapted from Table 8.

Table 6.4 Average hours per day spent on household activities by marital status, 2004.

	Total	Married spouse present	Other marital status
Female	2.25	2.71	1.72
Male	1.32	1.56	1.00
F/M	1.70	1.74	1.72

Source: U.S. Department of Labor, *American Time Use Survey, 2004*. Adapted from Tables 1 and 3.

6.2 Theoretical and Empirical Framework

To see how children and housework can affect wages, a general wage equation can be written as follows:

$$\ln W_{it} = X_{it}\beta + F_{it}\lambda + u_{it}, \tag{6.1}$$

$$u_{it} = \mu_i + \varepsilon_{it}, \tag{6.2}$$

where W represents the log of the real hourly wage of individual i at time t, X is a vector of human capital characteristics such as education and experience, and F is a vector of family factors such as number of children and time spent on household activities. The term u_{it} is the error term and consists of two components as indicated in Eq. (6.2). The first term, μ_i, is an individual-specific unobserved fixed effect, while the second term ε_{it} is a random error term.

For convenience in exposition, F represents all family factors as a single variable. Note that if family factors, such as children or housework, have a direct negative effect on wages, then we expect $\lambda < 0$. If, however, family factors are correlated with u_{it}, then OLS estimates of the effect of family factors on wage will be biased. There are two ways in which such a correlation can arise. First, the correlation could arise from the unobserved individual-specific fixed effect μ_i. For instance, if individuals with higher innate market productivity are less likely to either have children or spend considerable time on housework, then the coefficient on children or housework estimated by OLS will be biased downward. Second, children or housework and wages may be jointly endogenous. Workers with higher wages may be less likely to have children or may perform less housework, as they are more likely to purchase market substitutes for their housework time. The number of children or time on housework will be lower for higher-wage workers, so observed number of children or housework time will be correlated with the error term u_{it}. Once again OLS estimates will be biased downward, showing children or housework to have a greater negative effect on wages than true.

If panel data are available, fixed effects estimation can be used to eliminate the bias arising from unobserved individual-specific fixed effects.[2] If suitable instruments are available, instrumental variables (IV) techniques can be used to yield consistent estimates of the wage–housework relation no matter the nature of the correlation. Both approaches have been used to estimate the magnitude of the effect of family factors on earnings.

6.3 Empirical Evidence of a Family Pay Gap

The family gap in pay refers to lower hourly pay among women with children compared to women without children. Although childless women have average wages close to that of the average men (with or without children), the average wage of women with children is substantially below that of men (and correspondingly below that of childless women). Cross-sectional regressions controlling for individual

[2] Note however that greater ability might imply steeper age–earnings profiles, which would not be accounted for in fixed effects estimation, which restricts the role of unobserved ability to an intercept effect.

characteristics likewise often (but not always) find a negative effect of children on earnings. The source of this family gap is a matter of dispute. Both labor force participation and hours worked are lower for women with young children. Interruptions to work history alone with corresponding loss of human capital can cause a family gap. Goldin (1997) shows that even among college-educated women, women with children are less likely to work full time over a 3-year period than non-mothers and have lower earnings relative to men than non-mothers.

Data sets available when the earliest work on the gender pay gap was done lacked information on actual work history, and analyses would use potential experience as a proxy for work experience. Marital status and presence of children would be included as proxies for characteristics, such as labor force attachment, years out of the labor force, limitations on work location and hours, or investments in training. The first data set to include detailed work history for women is the 1967 NLS of mature women age 30–44 years. This survey includes retrospective work history information in segments of market and nonmarket time over the life cycle, reported relative to birth of children (such as market time before first child and home time after first child). Mincer and Polachek (1974) and Polachek (1975b) provide the first evidence on the family gap. Mincer and Polachek document time out of the market and the effects of such home time on wages, which vary considerably by marital status and number of children. Periods out of the labor force result in lower wages, which are interpreted in these papers as evidence that market skills depreciate during time out of the labor market. Notably, however, Mincer and Polachek find little direct effect of children on wages once detailed work experience is included in the regressions. Polachek shows how and why the gender gap varies with marital status and children, by segmenting the lifecycle to account for spacing of children. Having children in a shorter time period mitigates the cost to time out of the labor market.

While the various NLS surveys include respondents in specified age ranges, the PSID surveys household members of all ages. The 1976 wave of the PSID introduced extensive information on work history as well as on wages for non-household heads over the full age range. The data include very detailed information on work history and training, as well as on absenteeism by reason, whether job location or hours are restricted, and whether the individual plans to stop work for non-training reasons. Using the 1976 wave of the PSID, Hill (1979) finds that inclusion of these detailed measures of work experience eliminates the seeming child penalty.[3] However, other studies continue to find a negative effect of children on women's wages.

Rather than children causing lower wages, an alternative explanation is that less-productive women may select into childbearing. This selection may arise from unobserved heterogeneity between mothers and non-mothers, in that there may be a negative correlation between characteristics, such as career-orientation or motivation, and the desire to have children. One clue as to whether unobserved heterogeneity is likely to be important is derived from a comparison of wages and labor supply behavior of women before and after they have children. Unobserved heterogeneity would result in lower wages for women who eventually have children even before any children are born. But even here the evidence is mixed. Waldfogel (1998) finds no difference in pre-motherhood wages, but Lundberg and Rose (2000) find that women who eventually become mothers have wages 9 percentage points lower than those who never have children.

First difference and fixed effects estimates have been used to examine the role of unobserved heterogeneity, again yielding mixed findings. Korenman and Neumark (1992) use first difference estimates and find a smaller penalty thereby indicating the presence of unobserved heterogeneity. But their estimates using a sample of sisters continue to show a child penalty (Neumark and Korenman, 1994). Waldfogel (1997a) shows a wage penalty for women with children relative to

[3] Hill starts by presenting hourly wage regressions by sex and race controlling only for marital status, number of children, potential experience and its square, education, and whether south and city size. These regressions show a substantial marriage premium for white and black men of over 20 percent, no marital effects for women, and a statistically significant negative effect per child of 7 percent for white women only. Inclusion of actual work history and hours worked leaves the marriage effects largely unaffected but eliminates the negative children effect for white women. In fact, black women earn nearly 3 percent more per child. These findings suggest that in the absence of information on actual work experience, inclusion of the number of children in regressions serve as a proxy for work experience, but marriage does not proxy for work experience.

women without children, but estimated over a 12 or more year period, fixed effects and cross-sectional estimates yield similar penalties, suggesting unobserved heterogeneity is not important. Budig and England (2001) also find similar wage penalties for motherhood in fixed effects and cross-sectional estimates, with penalties of 2–10 percent for one child, and 5–13 percent for two or more.[4]

Rather than a wage penalty arising out of individual heterogeneity, giving birth may well be determined endogenously with both labor supply and earnings. For example, the time to give birth may be when wages are unusually low, or women with low market productivity may choose to have children. Instrumental variables methods have been used to examine endogenous fertility. Unsurprisingly, it is difficult to find instruments, and other approaches have been to use samples of twin births and to use gender composition of children (assuming that families strive to have mixed gender offspring).

An ideal experiment to avoid the problem of endogeneity of birth would be to randomly assign an infant to women. A more viable alternative is to examine the effect of multiple births on earning, as additional children are almost certainly exogenous. Jacobsen *et al.* (1999) undertake this analysis. Their study uses data drawn from the 1970 and 1980 PUMS of the Census. The sample size for 1970 was almost 500,000, with 3,445 twin births; for 1980 it was over 1.2 million, with 8,976 twin births. Three labor supply responses are estimated: (i) whether the mother worked for pay in the year preceding the Census; (ii) number of weeks worked in the year preceding the Census; and (iii) number of hours worked in the week preceding the Census. Representative findings with respect to labor supply are that the overall effect of twin first-birth lowers the probability of working by 1.4 (1.6) percentage points in 1969 (1979). But the impact is concentrated within the first 2 years after the twin birth, with probability of working 15.7 (11.5) percentage points lower than for those with single birth in 1969 (1979). The impact of twin birth relative to single birth disappears as children age. Similar

[4] Budig and England (2001) also examine whether mothers choose less energy-demanding occupations and conclude that such "mother-friendly" jobs explain little of the motherhood wage penalty.

patterns appear for weeks worked and hours worked per week, with the effects persisting somewhat longer as children age.

Jacobsen *et al.* find no evidence that twin birth leads to changes in occupation. But there is an adverse effect of twin birth on earnings that persists longer than does the effect of twin birth on labor supply, although even this negative effect on earnings disappears after the first child is 11 years or older. Instrumental variables estimates using twin birth as an instrument for number of children likewise show a negative effect of fertility on labor supply and earnings, but the magnitudes, while generally statistically significant, are small, as well as smaller in magnitude than without IV estimates. Furthermore, declining fertility from 1970 to 1980 accounts for only a small share of increased female labor supply. Analyses of twin births have the limitation that it does not allow examination of the effect of going from no children to one child (instead estimates the effect of going from zero to two children). Furthermore, the effect of twin birth is not necessarily equivalent to adding a net increase of one unplanned child to the household, but instead is more likely to affect the timing of births, lowering the number of additional children.

To examine whether negative selection into parenthood is responsible for the family gap, Lundberg and Rose (2000) examine the effect of continuous versus noncontinuous employment on wages using a sample of husband and wife couples in marriages of at least 5 years duration from the PSID 1980–1992. Most of the couples have children. The dependent variables are log of hourly wage and total hours worked during the year, and both random effects and fixed effects equations are estimated. Continuous participants are identified as those in which the wife participates continuously other than a year in which she gave birth. The random effects specification allows tracing out the age–wage and age–hours profile even for those whose childbirth status did not change.[5]

These estimates presented in Lundberg and Rose indicate dramatic differences between the continuously employed and the noncontinuous

[5] Although random effects will be inconsistent if the random effect is correlated with the regressors, the fixed effects estimates in this study are similar, giving credence to the random effects estimates.

samples. Furthermore, those who eventually give birth have lower earnings than non-childbearers even before giving birth, earning about 9 percent less than non-childbearers before birth, which increases to about 15 percent after birth. Thus, overall, the birth of a first child is associated with an additional 6 percentage point reduction in the mother's wage rate. But mothers who are continuously employed following first birth do not have a wage penalty in addition to the one they have relative to nonparents. This finding is consistent with Waldfogel's (1998) finding that those with job-protected maternity leave who return to work do not incur a wage loss. Fixed effects results show an overall wage reduction of 5 percent following childbirth, with no reduction for those continuously employed. In contrast, the wages of mothers who experience a substantial interruption following the birth of a first child fall by 25 percent.

Anderson *et al.* (2003) examine the role of timing of return to work in estimates of the motherhood penalty. They note that estimates of the effect of childbearing on wages may be obscured because there are differences in career orientation or return to same job of mothers who return to work quickly versus those who spend more time out of the labor market following birth. Hence, mothers who return to work quickly may be more career oriented and may not incur a penalty both by returning quickly and because of innate attributes, but when pooled with other mothers there may seem to be a penalty for all mothers. Also, wages may suffer because mothers spend less effort at work or because scheduling conflicts interact with work and reduce wages. Physical efforts and sleep interruptions are greatest when children are young, but older children pose more scheduling challenges. Thus, if the child penalty declines as children age, then effort may explain the penalty, but if it persists independently of children's age, then work schedule conflicts may be important.

To examine the effects of education and child's age on wages, Anderson *et al.* use data from the 1968–1988 NLSYW. Controlling for education, actual work experience and its square, age and its square, part-time employment, occupation, other adults in household, husband's income, and nonlabor income yields a wage penalty of 5.3 percent for one child and 7.6 percent for two or more children in cross-sectional estimates. Using the same control variables yields a penalty of 3 percent for one child and 5.7 percent for two or more children in fixed effects estimates that ignore the age of child when the mother returned to the workforce. Thus unobserved heterogeneity accounts for about one-third of the child penalty. Because the vast majority (74 percent) of the mothers in the sample return to the workforce when their youngest child is 2 years old or younger, the fixed effects estimates for those in this group are similar to the estimates for the entire sample, and there is no evidence of a penalty for those returning to the workforce when the child is older.

Stratifying the sample by the age of youngest child at return to the workforce and mapping out the wage pattern as the child(ren) age shows that the penalty is largest at the time the mother of preschool age children returns to work, and the penalty tapers off. Women who return to work when the youngest child is 0–2 years experience a penalty of 2.6 percent when the child is that age, but this drops to 1 percent when the child is 3–5 years and to less than 1 percent when ages 6–10 years, becoming insignificant thereafter. The child penalty for those returning to work when the child is 3–5 years incur a penalty of 3.9 percent when the child is that age, but no penalty thereafter, while there is no penalty for those returning when the child is age 6–17 years.

One interpretation of these findings is that adjustment costs are highest shortly after return to work, as well as with a job matching explanation in which the initial time period after returning to work is the time when a preferred match is being sought. But the tapering off of any wage penalty over time is also consistent with the hypothesis that work effort is greatest among women with younger children. Stratification by education indicates that in fixed effects estimates, penalties are incurred only among those who are high school graduates or have some college, but there is no penalty among those with less than high school or college graduates. The authors interpret this as evidence against the work effort hypothesis, arguing that work effort should be greatest among the most educated.

There is a range of possible labor supply responses to the presence of children. Some mothers take minimal time off, and the passage of the Family and Medical Leave Act (FMLA) formalized the conditions in which returning to the original employer was likely. Using panel data from the NLSY79 and NLSYW, Waldfogel (1998) finds that women who return to their employer within 12 months after a recent birth have wages 11–12 percent higher than women who did not return so quickly, due to greater experience and work tenure. Coverage by maternity leave also results in higher wages upon return. Those who had maternity coverage and return to their employer do not suffer any wage loss (Waldfogel, 1997b).

Other women exit for longer periods or may return to part-time jobs or jobs in a different occupation that may provide more flexibility or require less effort (and may have lower wages because of compensating differentials). Presumably only those women whose opportunity cost at home is less than their wage rate return to the labor market at the time childcare demands are extensive, so such selection would tend to mitigate the child pay gap. Studies taking into account the actual effect on labor supply in terms of elapsed time off or hours worked may yield different conclusions.

Most studies estimate the family gap using women in a wide range of occupations. It is of interest to see whether highly educated women in professions also experience a motherhood penalty. Sasser (2005) uses data from the American Medical Association Young Physician's Survey to examine whether earnings of physicians fall after childbirth, and if so, whether it is due to reduced hours or lower productivity. Prior to marriage or to having children, women who later married or became mothers had higher earnings than those who did not marry or have children.[6] However, after marriage or children, a considerable pay gap develops as these women reduce their hours of work.

To examine effort reduction versus simply hours reduction, Sasser compares the child gap in hourly wage and in annual earnings. Simply reducing hours worked would reduce annual earnings but not hourly pay, but reducing effort would reduce both. If employer discrimination against those with family responsibilities plays a role, then the gap should be greater for those who are employees than those who are

[6] This finding differs from Lundberg and Rose (2000) who show lower pre-child earnings for eventual mothers within a broad range of occupations.

self-employed. Sasser finds that the bulk of the gap is due to reduction in annual hours rather than in reduced effort per hour work in that there is no significant difference in hourly earnings among women based on number of children. However, children influence annual hours worked. There is no difference between males and females in the number of patients seen per hour, so differences in productivity do not seem to be an important determinant of the gap. The gender pay gap is the same or even greater when stratifying by self-employed and employee physicians, suggesting that employer discrimination is probably not important (nor would be customer discrimination as physicians' marital and parental status are unlikely to be observed).

6.4 Effect of Housework on Earnings

There is substantial literature documenting a negative relation between housework and wages. This effect appears consistently for women across a variety of data sets. Coverman (1983) uses the 1977 Quality of Employment Survey, Hersch (1985) uses data on piece rate workers, Shelton and Firestone (1989) use the 1981 Time Use Survey, Hersch (1991c) and Stratton (2001) a regional wage survey collected by Hersch, Hersch (1991b), Hersch and Stratton (1997), and Hundley (2000) the PSID,[7] Noonan (2001) and Hersch and Stratton (2002) use data from the National Survey of Families and Households, Phipps *et al.* (2001) use data from the 1995 Statistics Canada General Social Survey, Bonke *et al.* (2003) use data from the 1987 Danish Time Use Survey, and Keith and Malone (2005) use data from the PSID. The magnitudes of the effect of housework time on wages tend to be fairly small but are statistically significant. Estimates for men largely fail to find a significant relation between wages and housework or find a much smaller effect.

Many of these studies estimate wage equations by OLS and control for standard human capital measures. Similar concerns about endogeneity and unobserved heterogeneity arise here as with estimates of the effect of children on wages. For example, individuals receiving higher

[7] Hundley examines the effect of housework on the pay gap in self-employed workers.

market wages may be more likely to hire household help. As such, a wage equation including controls for housework may yield biased and inconsistent parameter estimates. Furthermore, the negative housework effect may be spurious due to omitted fixed effects if individuals doing much housework are innately less productive at market work. Housework time may be a proxy for some individual specific characteristic such as "taste for market employment" or "market ambition."

Hersch and Stratton (1997) examine whether the housework–wage effect is due to unobserved heterogeneity or endogeneity using panel data from the 1979–1987 PSID. Fixed effects estimates indicate that housework time continues to have a significant negative effect upon wages for married women in fixed effects results, although the magnitude is about one-third as that estimated using OLS. While OLS estimates for men indicate a significant negative effect of housework on wages for men, there is no effect of housework on wages for men in a fixed effects model. However, housework time is almost invariant over time for men. Furthermore, the nature of the question on housework available on the PSID is likely to result in particularly weak estimates of housework time for men.[8] If reported differences in housework for men over time are primarily due to measurement error, then the housework coefficient would be biased toward zero for men, particularly in the fixed effects specification. Estimation with better housework data (such as that available in the ATUS) could help identify if there is a negative relation between housework and wages for men that is not driven by individual specific effects.

To address concerns about bias due to possible joint endogeneity between housework time and wages, Hersch and Stratton also estimate instrumental variables equations using alternative instrument sets to establish robustness, and consistently find a negative and statistically

[8] The housework question on the PSID asks: "About how much time do (you or your spouse) spend on housework in an average week? I mean time spent cooking, cleaning, and doing other work around the house." The question does not specifically request information on childcare, but as the presence of children adds 5 hours per week on average to women's housework time (and less than 1 hour to men's average), it is likely that activities such as extra laundry and cleaning associated with children are included in the report of housework time. Comparison to the ATUS diary information supports this interpretation once the youngest household child is over age 6 years.

significant effect of housework on wages for women, although the effect for men is neither stable nor statistically significant. These results confirm that coefficient estimates from IV regressions are largely similar to those of OLS. Most importantly, there is strong evidence that housework is exogenous, giving further credence to the reliability of OLS estimates.

The fixed effects and instrumental variables results indicate that the OLS finding of a negative effect of housework on wages is genuine, at least for women, and endogeneity does not seem to be a fatal problem. Comparison of fixed effects to IV results suggests that measurement error is likely to bias toward zero the estimated effects.

The general failure to find a relation between housework and wages for men and the results reported in Hersch (1991c) that only housework performed on job days yields a negative effect of housework on wages for women suggest that the relation between housework and wages may not be a simple relation between total time and wages. There may be some threshold of time that must be crossed before housework affects wages, or the effect of housework on wages may differ by type of housework, or the timing of housework rather than the total amount of housework may influence the relation.

Observing the vast disparity between men and women in total housework time suggests that although relatively small amounts of time on household activities undertaken by men can easily fit into the day and will not be fatiguing or disruptive, and can even be enjoyable, wages may be affected adversely by the large quantity performed by employed women. Hersch and Stratton (1997) find some evidence in support of a threshold effect for women. Women's wages are not affected by up to ten hours of housework per week, with the negative effect of housework kicking in after this point. There is no support, however, for a threshold effect of housework time for men, as the coefficients are not significantly different from each other over the range of housework time reported by men.

Rather than housework of any kind influencing wages, the type of housework may matter. Household chores such as cooking, cleaning, and laundry may affect wages, while home maintenance that can often be deferred may not. As women are far more likely to be responsible for routine activities performed almost daily, such as cooking and cleaning, and men are more likely to be responsible for repairs and yard work, this may explain the smaller or insignificant effect of housework on men's wages.

To see whether the effect on wages of housework time is affected by marital status and to see whether type of housework matters, Hersch and Stratton (2002) use data from the National Survey of Families and Households (NSFH). The NSFH requests respondents and their spouses to report on time spent on nine different household activities. Hersch and Stratton group these activities into three categories reflecting the observed gender stratification of activities: (i) "Typically female" activities include meal preparation, washing dishes, cleaning, shopping for groceries and other household goods, and laundry; (ii) "Typically male" activities include outdoor and maintenance activities and auto repair; (iii) "Neutral activities," on which both men and women spend similar amounts of time, include bill paying and driving others.

Hersch and Stratton's analysis shows that the effect of housework on wages does not differ by marital status. Housework time primarily influences wages only for women, and the magnitude of the effect is similar across all marital statuses. Second, type of housework matters considerably. Time spent on typically female housework has a significant effect on women's wages and is even marginally significant for married men. But with the exception of the effect of neutral housework on earnings for not-married men, no other type of housework has an influence on wages.[9]

Finding that it is typically female housework that influences wages, coupled with the finding in Hersch (1991c) that it is housework on job days that influences wages, suggest that it is timing and/or limited effort during the workday that affects wages.

The results in Hersch and Stratton (1997) indicate that although the magnitude of the effect of housework on wages is fairly small, with each additional hour of housework reducing hourly wage by only about 4–5 cents per hour, inclusion of housework in the wage equation explains a

[9] Instrumental variables estimates for women also show a negative relation between housework and wages, but Hersch and Stratton (2002) are not able to reject the hypothesis that housework is exogenous for both men and women.

large component of the gender wage gap. Estimates that do not control for housework explain 27–30 percent of gender wage gap. Inclusion of time on housework increases the explanatory power of the observables to 38 percent. Furthermore, lowering women's housework time would have a large effect on earnings. Decreasing housework to men's average would raise wages to the same level as increasing tenure to men's average. Using data from the NSFH, Hersch and Stratton (2002) perform a similar analysis using both married and not-married workers and find that inclusion in the wage equation of housework time increases the explained component of the gender wage gap by about 14 percentage points, from 29.1 percent when housework is excluded, to 43.4 percent.

Keith and Malone (2005) extend the analysis of Hersch and Stratton (1997) to examine whether the effect of housework on wages varies over the life cycle. They use PSID data for 1983–1993. The sample is comprised of employed married men and women, who are stratified into three age groups: ages 20–24, 35–49, and 50–65 years. OLS estimates indicate the housework time has a significant negative effect on wages for all age groups and for both men and women. The effect for men disappears in fixed effects estimates and in Hausman–Taylor IV (HTIV) estimates, but continues to show a negative effect for women, with the effect for women in the oldest age group just failing to reach significance at the 10 percent level in fixed effects estimates. The magnitude of the wage penalty for women in the youngest age group is nearly twice the size of the penalty of the middle-age group, suggesting that life cycle has an influence. Housework demands are most disruptive when women are younger, perhaps because younger women are also more likely to have young children. Inclusion of housework increases the explained component of the wage gap between men and women of the same age group, with the magnitude differing based on whether OLS or HTIV estimates are used. Overall, Keith and Malone report that housework time contributes 3–10 percent of the explained portion of the gap.

7

Compensating Differentials

The theory of compensating differentials maintains that workers receive premium pay for undesirable work characteristics, such as fatality or injury risks, and receive lower pay for attractive characteristics. Compensating differentials for work characteristics provide an attractive interpretation of the gender pay gap. The working conditions in jobs held by women on average tend to be in safer and more pleasant work environments, as women are less likely than men to be in blue-collar jobs or jobs requiring outdoor work or physical demands. Women may choose jobs with working conditions that are compatible with heavy household responsibilities, such as with shorter commutes or flexible schedules. Under the theory of compensating differentials, the pay disparity arises because of gender differences in preferences about working conditions.

Most of the empirical literature has estimated wage–risk tradeoffs. Indeed, research shows generally little support for compensating differentials for working conditions other than fatality or injury risk. The general failure to find compensating differentials for work characteristics other than risk has bearing on whether compensating differentials are likely to explain a substantial share of the gender pay disparity.

7.1 Statistics on Fatalities, Injuries, and Flexible Schedules

Table 7.1 gives an overview of occupational fatalities and causes by sex. Job fatalities are quite rare events, with an all-worker fatality rate of 4.1 per 100,000 workers in 2004. Women comprise only 7.2 percent of the total fatalities. Relative to men, women are disproportionately more likely to die on the job from assault or violent act.

Table 7.2 reports the number of nonfatal occupational injuries and the corresponding female share. Nonfatal injuries are fairly common, with an overall incidence rate of 4.8 cases per 100 equivalent full-time workers in 2004. In contrast to fatalities, women are considerably more likely to suffer nonfatal injuries or illness involving days away from work.

Flexible work schedules are an amenity that may warrant lower pay as a compensating differential. Tables 7.3 and 7.4 provide statistics on trends in flexible schedules among full-time workers. Workers are defined as having a flexible schedule if they answer yes to the CPS supplement question, “Do you have flexible work hours that allow you to vary or make changes in the time you begin and end work?” Note the large increase in workers with a flexible schedule since 1985, the year the CPS initiated questions on flexibility in schedules. Women with considerable family responsibilities would seem to prefer such schedules. Yet, as shown in Table 7.3, men are actually more likely to have a flexible schedule. Furthermore, as shown in Table 7.4, the likelihood of having a flexible schedule is largely unrelated to the presence or age of children. The statistics in these tables suggest that even if workers receive lower pay for flexibility, since men are more likely to have flexibility in their jobs than women, the possibility that women prefer flexibility because of family responsibilities will not translate into a substantial reduction in the unexplained component of the pay gap.

7.2 Compensating Differentials for Fatality or Injury Risk

There is extensive evidence that women are more risk averse than are men, which itself implies that women may have different preferences that result in women choosing jobs with less risk of physical injury or

Table 7.1 Fatal occupational injuries and event or exposure, 2004.

	Total fatalities	Transportation incidents	Assaults and violent acts	Contact with objects and equipment	Falls	Exposure to harmful substances or environments	Fires and explosions
Total	5703	2460	795	1004	815	459	159
Female	411	187	121	26	37	27	10
Male	5292	2273	674	978	778	432	149
Female share of total	7.2	7.6	15.2	2.6	4.5	5.9	6.3

Source: U.S. Department of Labor, *Census of Fatal Occupational Injuries*. Available at www.bls.gov/iif/oshwc/cfoi/cftb0202.pdf.

Table 7.2 Nonfatal occupational injuries and illnesses involving days away from work.

	Total	Total goods producing	Total service producing	Median days away from work
Total	1,259,320	408,400	850,930	7
Female	425,470	60,030	365,440	7
Male	829,300	348,220	481,090	8
Female share of total	33.8	14.7	42.9	

Source: U.S. Department of Labor, *Workplace Injuries and Illnesses in 2004*. Available at http://www.bls.gov/news.release/pdf/osh2.pdf. Adapted from Tables 1 and 8.

Table 7.3 Percent with flexible schedules, full-time wage and salary workers, selected years.

	May 1985	May 1997	May 2004
Female	11.3	26.2	26.7
Male	13.1	28.6	28.1
F/M %	86.3	91.6	95.0

Source: U.S. Department of Labor, *Workers in Flexible and Shift Schedules in May 2004*. Available at http://www.bls.gov/news.release/pdf/flex.pdf. Adapted from Table A.

Table 7.4 Percent with flexible schedules by age of youngest child, full-time wage and salary workers, 2004.

	Youngest child under 6 years	Youngest child 6–17 years	None under 18 years
Female	26.4	25.5	27.1
Male	30.2	29.1	27.1
F/M %	87.4	87.6	100.0

Source: U.S. Department of Labor, *Workers in Flexible and Shift Schedules in May 2004*. Available at http://www.bls.gov/news.release/pdf/flex.pdf. Adapted from Table 1.

death. Using data from the 1987 National Medical Expenditure Survey (NMES), Hersch (1996) shows that women make safer health choices than men with respect to smoking, wearing a seatbelt, flossing, brushing teeth, and checking blood pressure. Jianakoplos and Bernasek (1998) find evidence that women are more risk averse than men in their financial decisions using data from the 1989 Survey of Consumer Finances. DeLeire and Levy (2004) estimate conditional logit models of occupational choice at the two-digit level, showing that greater fatality risk deters employment in risky occupations for women more than for men, and that single parents, both male and female, are less likely to sort into risky jobs.

Until recently, job risk measures were available only at the industry level, hence there was no way to distinguish between risks faced by, say, male miners and female office workers in the mining industry. This measurement error led most researchers who assumed women were employed in safe jobs to exclude female workers from any analysis of compensating differentials for injury or death risk, as estimates based on samples including women failed to find a significant wage–risk premium. In 1993 the BLS began recording gender, occupation, and age range associated with fatalities and nonfatal injuries. Using these newly available data, Hersch (1998) reports that adjusted for differences in labor supply, women are 76 percent as likely as men to have a lost workday injury. Within white-collar occupations, the injury rate for women is 80 percent higher than for men. Furthermore, women receive a substantial compensating differential for gender-specific job risk, of a magnitude similar to blue-collar men. In contrast, there is almost no evidence that white-collar men receive a compensating differential for job risk. Thus, inclusion of job injury risk will not narrow the explained share of the gender pay gap but may instead increase it.

Leeth and Ruser (2003) perform an analysis similar to Hersch (1998) by race as well as by gender, adding to the wage equation gender-specific and race-specific fatality rates as well as injury rates, matched by three-digit occupation. Using data for 1996–1998, they find that men receive a premium for fatality risk. There is inconsistent or insignificant evidence that women also receive a premium for fatality risk. Both male and female workers receive a wage premium for nonfatal injury risk, with the premium substantially higher for women. Neither male nor female workers receive a premium for risk of death in white-collar jobs, and although there is some evidence that males in blue-collar jobs receive a premium for fatality risk, there is only weak evidence that females in blue-collar jobs do as well.

7.3 Compensating Differentials for Working Conditions Other Than Risk

Refer again to a general wage equation,

$$\ln W_{it} = X_{it}\beta + HW_{it}\gamma + J_t\alpha + u_{it}, \tag{7.1}$$

where W represents the log of the real hourly wage of individual i at time t, X is a vector of human capital characteristics, and HW is time spent on household activities and may be measured as total time over some period, or on weekdays and weekends, or divided into time spent on specific types of activities, such as cleaning and yard work. J is a vector of job attributes that may warrant a compensating differential. Time spent on housework is explicitly introduced to recognize that men and women may have different preferences over working conditions because of differences in household responsibilities. The fixed effects and IV results of Hersch and Stratton (1997) imply that the error term in this equation is not correlated with the explanatory variables, hence we assume here that the error term u_{it} is random and OLS estimation is appropriate. OLS is also the predominant method of estimation throughout the literature.

The specification above allows us to examine whether the estimated inverse housework–wage relation arises from failure to control for working conditions. The only paper that examines both the role of housework and working conditions is Hersch (1991c). Hersch uses self-collected data from a sample of manufacturing workers who report information on housework and childcare time, working conditions, and job effort, as well as on wages and human capital characteristics. The housework and childcare questions request respondents to report how much time they spent separately on housework and on childcare on both job days and non-job days. Respondents report the nonpecuniary characteristics of their jobs, such as whether they are exposed to unsafe working conditions or bad weather, whether their job requires physical exertion, and whether their job allows for individual discretion over how to perform the job and whether the job is repetitive or stressful. The working conditions provided by this study have the considerable advantage of being individual-specific rather than imputed from industry or occupational means (such as the DOT), which is the method most widely used to measure working conditions (e.g., Macpherson and Hirsch, 1995).

In contrast to the literature of the time, Hersch's (1991c) wage analysis indicates substantial evidence of compensating differentials for a wide range of working conditions. Wages are higher for those with more decision-making authority and freedom to decide how to work, as well as for those with more job stress. Repetitive jobs are associated with lower pay, reflecting the lesser mental demands of such work. Inclusion of working conditions substantially increases the explanatory power of the wage equations. Yet inclusion of working conditions did not unambiguously reduce the unexplained wage gap between men and women.[1] Furthermore, the effect of housework on wages, as well as the effect of children on wages, is altered only slightly by the inclusion of working conditions in the equation, suggesting that any correlation between household responsibilities and working conditions is minor.

Flexible schedules would seem to be a desirable working condition warranting lower pay as a compensating differential. But offsetting any negative wage effect is the possibility that flexibility makes workers more productive. Gariety and Shaffer (2001) use CPS data on flexible schedules reported in supplements in 1989 and 1997 to estimate wage equations controlling for whether a worker has a flexible schedule, as well as controlling for the reason such as transportation or because of family and child responsibilities. The evidence does not provide evidence that flexibility is a job benefit warranting lower pay for women. In both years women receive a positive wage premium for flexibility, as did men in the second year of data. Women's preference for jobs with greater flexibility, therefore, cannot explain the gender pay disparity.

[1] There is an increase in the explained component using the female coefficients but not the male coefficients.

8

Differences in Content of Education

Education is a key human capital investment. Although questions remain about whether education enhances productivity or signals that an individual has greater innate ability, regression analyses invariably show that education has a positive and substantial effect on earnings. In contrast to years of work experience, there has long been little disparity in educational achievement by sex, or if any, women have had an edge. Women have been more likely to be high school graduates, and in recent years more women than men have earned bachelor's degrees, with men somewhat but not dramatically more likely than women to earn graduate degrees. For example, in 2001–2002, women were awarded 57.4 percent of bachelor's degrees, 46.3 percent of doctorates, and 47.3 percent of first professional degrees.[1] In wage decompositions, with little difference in average years of education between men and women, even greatly larger returns to education for men will have a small impact on explaining gender disparities in pay.

However, men and women have tended to have very different majors in college, and even in high school acquire different schooling. In particular,

[1] U.S. Department of Education, *National Center for Education Statistics, Integrated Postsecondary Education Data System*, Fall 2002, Tables 265, 271, and 274.

there is evidence that returns to mathematical and scientific education are higher than in other disciplines, and women have been underrepresented in these disciplines. There are several possible reasons why men and women may choose different majors. Individuals choose majors by comparing costs and benefits. Expectations of intermittent labor force participation would reduce the benefits of fields, such as science, that require substantial on the job training or have a high rate of depreciation of knowledge.[2] As the tables below show, the gender disparity in fields has narrowed over time, and if noncontinuous participation is a primary reason for the gender disparity in majors, the gap should narrow even more as women are in the labor force more continuously.

Another possibility is that women have lower ability in male disciplines or differ in preferences so that they choose traditionally female disciplines. Greater ability in the major will lower the costs of investment, so those with mathematics aptitude should major in more quantitative fields. The average math SAT score among boys is higher than the average score for girls by about 50 points, although boys and girls have similar verbal SAT scores. As the studies discussed below show, however, controlling for standardized tests scores does not eliminate the unexplained gender disparity in either choice of majors or earnings. Still another possibility is that certain predominantly male majors are unfriendly enough to women that even entry is limited by discrimination. A related reason is that the returns to fields may be lower for women in predominantly male fields than for men in the same fields.

8.1 Trends in Educational Attainment and College Majors

Table 8.1 shows the educational attainment among those in the labor force in 1970 and 2004. College educated workers were the minority of the labor force in 1970. Women in the labor force at that time were less likely than men to have a college degree, but were more likely to be a high school graduate. By 2004, few labor force participants are not high school graduates, and a greater share of women than men have at least some college or are college graduates.

[2] An example given by Turner and Bowen (1999) is that knowledge of Shakespeare may provide more opportunities than knowledge of the nearly obsolete software program Cobol.

Table 8.1 Percent distribution of highest educational attainment of labor force 25–64 years of age, 1970 and 2004.

	Less than 4 years high school/less than high school diploma	4 years high school/high school graduate	Some college and associate degree	4 years or more college/college graduates and higher degrees
1970				
Female	33.5	44.3	10.9	11.2
Male	37.5	34.5	12.2	15.7
2004				
Female	7.7	29.4	30.2	32.6
Male	11.5	30.7	25.6	32.3

Note: The CPS educational category definitions were changed in 1992.
Source: U.S. Department of Labor, *Women in the Labor Force: A Databook (2005)*. Adapted from Table 9.

Table 8.2 Women's earnings as a percent of men's, median usual weekly earnings of full-time wage and salary workers 25 years and over by educational attainment.

	1979	1980	1990	2000	2004
Total	62.1	62.7	72.1	74.5	78.7
Less than high school diploma	60.2	61.3	68.8	74.9	74.9
High school graduate	60.0	61.3	68.6	71.2	75.6
Some college or associate degree	64.0	64.5	72.8	73.1	75.8
Bachelor's degree or higher	66.6	67.8	72.2	74.1	75.2

Source: U.S. Department of Labor, *Highlights of Women's Earnings in 2004* (2005). Adapted from Table 14.

Table 8.2 shows women's earnings as a percent of men's with the same education for selected years from 1979 to 2004. By 2004 there is little difference by education in the female to male earnings ratio. In fact, relative wage growth has been the slowest for women with college degrees or higher between 1979 and 2004.

Table 8.3 reports the average verbal and math SAT scores for males and females entering college classes in the years 1970, 1980, 1990, and 2002. Verbal scores are similar for males and females. Female math scores are on average below the male scores, ranging from 92 to 94 percent of average male scores. Why women have lower average SAT scores is not fully understood, but it is worthwhile noting that more women than men attend college so in part the average scores may reflect inclusion of a greater share nonmathematical-oriented college-bound females than males.

Table 8.3 Average SAT scores of entering college classes, selected years.

	1970	1980	1990	2002
Verbal (all)	537	502	500	504
Female	538	498	496	502
Male	536	506	505	507
F/M %	100.4	98.4	98.2	99.0
Math (all)	512	492	501	516
Female	493	473	483	500
Male	531	515	521	534
F/M %	92.8	91.8	92.7	93.6

Source: The College Board, available at www.collegeboard.com/prod_downloads/about/news_info/cbsenior/yr2002/pdf/table2.pdf.

Table 8.4 Number of earned degrees by level of degree, selected years.

	1969–1970	1979–1980	1989–1990	1999–2000
Associate degrees total	206,023	400,910	455,102	564,933
Female	88,591	217,173	263,907	340,212
Male	117,432	183,737	191,195	224,721
Female percent of total	43.0	54.2	58.0	60.2
Bachelor's degrees total	792,316	929,417	1,051,344	1,237,875
Female	341,219	455,806	559,648	707,508
Male	451,097	473,611	491,696	530,367
Female percent of total	43.1	49.0	53.2	57.2
Master's degrees total	208,291	298,081	324,301	457,056
Female	82,667	147,332	170,648	265,264
Male	125,624	150,749	153,653	191,792
Female percent of total	39.7	49.4	52.6	58.0
First-professional degrees total	34,918	70,131	70,988	80,057
Female	1,841	17,415	27,027	35,818
Male	33,077	52,716	43,961	44,239
Female percent of total	5.3	24.8	38.1	44.7
Doctor's degrees total	29,866	32,615	38,371	44,808
Female	3,976	9,672	13,970	19,780
Male	25,890	22,943	24,401	25,028
Female percent of total	13.3	29.7	36.4	44.1

Source: U.S. Department of Education, *Digest of Education Statistics 2003.* Adapted from Table 249. Doctor's degrees include Ph.D., Ed.D., and comparable degrees at the doctoral level, and excludes first-professional such as M.D., D.D.S., and law degrees.

Table 8.4 shows the trend in female share of degrees over the years 1969–1970 to 1999–2000. Women received somewhat fewer than half of the associate, bachelor's, and master's degrees in 1969–1970, and somewhat more than half of these degrees by 1999–2000. Most dramatic is the large upsurge in the share of women receiving professional degrees and doctorates. In 1969–1970, only 5 percent of professional degrees and 13 percent of doctorates were awarded to women. By 1999–2000, 45 percent of professional degrees and 44 percent of doctorates were awarded to women.

Table 8.5 shows trends in degrees by field over the period 1970–1971 and 2001–2002. Over the 30-year period, business moved from being an almost exclusively male major to one in which half of the bachelor's degrees are awarded to women. Psychology, education and health professions and related sciences have long been popular among female students, and while there is little trend among women in education or in health professions, psychology moved from a field in which fewer than half of the degrees were awarded to women to one in which women are awarded the majority of the degrees at all levels. Despite women's lower average math SAT scores, a large share of mathematics majors are female, with the rise in the female share of doctorates most notable. Even engineering, long a male stronghold, has experienced a large increase in the share of female majors, going from nearly nonexistent in 1970 to about one in five by 2001.

8.2 Choice of College Major and Effects on the Pay Gap

In an early study of sex differences in choice of college major, Polachek (1978) posits a human capital investment model that implies that women select college majors with lower penalties to labor force intermittency. Polachek uses data from two sources: Explorations in Equality of Opportunity 1955–1970, a sample of high school sophomores surveyed in 1955 and resurveyed in 1970, and the National Longitudinal Study of the High School Class of 1972 (NLS72), a sample who were surveyed as college freshman in 1973. Polachek examines the choice of college major controlling for a variety of characteristics including aptitude measured by standardized test scores, courses taken in high school, and parents' education, as well as extensive attitudinal or preference characteristics, such as whether the respondent attended college because college graduates earn more, in order to develop socially, to marry well, and so forth. Majors are grouped in nine standard

Table 8.5 Number of earned degrees by selected fields and female share of total, 1970–1971 and 2001–2002.

	1970–1971			2001–2002		
	Bachelor's degrees	Master's degrees	Doctor's degrees	Bachelor's degrees	Master's degrees	Doctor's degrees
Business	114,729	25,977	757	281,330	120,785	1,158
Female	10,454	1,010	21	140,764	49,628	410
Male	104,275	24,967	736	140,566	71,157	748
Female share	9.1	3.9	2.8	50.0	41.1	35.4
Computer and information sciences	2,388	1,588	128	47,299	16,113	750
Female	324	164	3	13,051	5,360	171
Male	2,064	1,424	125	34,248	10,753	579
Female share	13.6	10.3	2.3	27.6	33.3	22.8
Education	176,307	87,666	6,041	106,383	136,579	6,967
Female	131,411	49,301	1,270	82,332	104,407	4,632
Male	44,896	38,365	4,771	24,051	32,172	2,335
Female share	74.5	56.2	21.0	77.4	76.4	66.5
Engineering	50,046	16,443	3,638	73,964	26,920	5,210
Female	400	185	23	13,974	5,753	900
Male	49,646	16,258	3,615	59,990	21,167	4,310
Female share	0.8	1.1	0.05	18.9	21.4	17.3
Health professions and related sciences	25,226	5,749	466	70,517	43,644	3,523
Female	19,438	3,182	77	60,260	33,847	2,230
Male	5,788	2,567	389	10,257	9,797	1,293
Female share	77.1	55.3	16.5	85.5	77.6	63.3
Mathematics	24,937	5,695	1,249	12,395	3,487	958
Female	9,439	1,546	95	5,787	1,478	278
Male	15,498	4,149	1,154	6,608	2,009	680
Female share	37.9	27.1	7.6	46.7	42.4	29.0
Psychology	38,187	5,717	2,144	76,671	14,888	4,341
Female	16,960	2,322	515	59,396	11,371	2,962
Male	21,227	3,395	1,629	17,275	3,517	1,379
Female share	44.4	40.6	24.0	77.5	76.4	68.2

Source: U.S. Department of Education, *Digest of Education Statistics 2003*. Adapted from Tables 280, 282, 283, 284, 289, 290, 293.

categories (e.g., business, education, and engineering) and choice of major is estimated by multivariate logit. The results accord with expectations, showing that those with greater quantitative ability are more likely to major in math, science, or engineering relative to humanities. While one might expect that such extensive controls for background and preferences would result in an insignificant effect of sex on choice of major, Polachek does not find this to be the case. However, the unexplained effect of sex on choice of college major declines somewhat between the first period in the 1950s and the second period in the 1970s.

Additional information on the importance of standardized tests on choice of major is provided by Turner and Bowen (1999), who use data on all students entering twelve selective colleges in 1951, 1976, and 1989 in the College and Beyond data set. Turner and Bowen show that even women with high math SAT scores are more likely than men to choose nonquantitative majors such as life sciences and humanities than engineering, math, and physical sciences. Differences in SAT scores vary by major, but overall account for less than half the gender gap in choice of major and explain much less of the disparity in economics and psychology. Furthermore, the gap between men and women in choice of majors did not shrink between 1976 and 1989, and in fact rose in psychology and life sciences.

Salaries vary considerably by college major. Of interest is whether a gender pay disparity remains after controlling for major. Studies have used individual data as well as aggregated data on recently hired college graduates.

Brown and Corcoran (1997) show that college major explains a considerable component of the pay disparity among college graduates, but content of coursework does not explain differences among those with high school degrees or with some college. Among college graduates, including college major in addition to measures of experience raises the explained component of the 1984 pay disparity from about half to two-thirds in analyses based on Survey of Income Program Participants (SIPP) data. Corresponding calculations for college graduates from the NLS72 in the 1986 follow-up raises the explained component to over half from 20 percent. The age range in the SIPP is unrestricted, and those in the NLS72 are all in their early 30s when resurveyed in 1986.

Based on the NLS72 data, Brown and Corcoran find that women college graduates receive a higher return than men in humanities and engineering and a lower return in biology, math, and physical sciences. Also of interest is their finding that controlling for high school test scores as measures of ability contributes nothing to the explained gender pay differential. Furthermore, among those who are not college graduates, controlling for specific high school courses or major when attended college accounts for no difference, or at most a small difference, in the gender pay disparity. Since only one-third of those in the labor market are college graduates, this suggests that despite gender differences in high school course work, such differences are not important determinants of the pay disparity, a point further supported by the finding that a considerable unexplained gap remains even after controlling for college major among college graduates.

Instead of analyzing individual data, Paglin and Rufolo (1990) compare starting salary offers by majors with mean GRE scores in that major. The GRE quantitative score (GRE-Q) is highly positively correlated with starting salary offers reported by the College Placement Council (now called the National Association of Colleges and Employers). The GRE verbal score is not correlated with starting salary offers. Paglin and Rufolo present descriptive statistics showing a skewed distribution of GRE-Q by sex, with women in lower GRE-Q ranges. Assuming that students select into majors in which they have a comparative advantage, Paglin and Rufolo interpret their findings as showing that fields with a high proportion of women are lower paying because these are fields in which human capital can be produced with lesser amounts of the scarce resource of quantitative ability. Their study shows no remaining gender pay disparity after accounting for major among new college graduates. Also using data from the National Association of Colleges and Employers data set, McDonald and Thornton (forthcoming) find that college major explains up to 95 percent of the gap in starting salary offers over the years 1974–2001.[3] The data set reports average starting salaries by sex

[3] McDonald and Thornton (forthcoming) provides a valuable survey of the literature on the role of college major in explaining the gender pay gap.

divided into nearly 80 different majors. However, the samples used in these papers may not be representative, as the data are derived from salary offers made to students recruited through campus college placement centers.

Weinberger (1999) points out that disproportionately fewer women than men were recruited through campus college placement centers, which raises concerns about the representativeness of the samples examined by Paglin and Rufolo (1990) and McDonald and Thornton (forthcoming). Weinberger performs an analysis similar to that of Paglin and Rufolo using data from the 1985 Survey of Recent College Graduates who are age 30 or younger. Controlling for college GPA and average GRE-Q by graduates in the major, Weinberger finds that a 9 percent gender pay gap remains and that the gap does not vary by whether the major is technical or not.

In sum, despite historic differences in choices of college major and the propensity of women to choose less quantitative majors, controlling for college major does not eliminate the gender pay disparity.

9

Evidence on Discrimination Based on Observed Productivity or Stock Market Response

Because it is always possible that any unexplained gap is due to differences in productivity, one potentially attractive approach would be to compare wage disparities to productivity disparities using data reporting both individual wages and direct measures of productivity. The advantage of such an approach is that although we know we may have omitted productivity characteristics, such omitted characteristics should affect both wages and productivity in the same manner. Evidence showing wage disparities that are greater than productivity disparities are consistent with discrimination.

Of course, measures of individual productivity are rare. Firm level data can also be used to study discrimination. Using the Worker Establishment Characteristics Database (WECD), a matched employer–employee data set of manufacturing establishments, Hellerstein *et al.* (1999) compare relative marginal productivity of females and males to relative wages. This study finds lower marginal productivity for females than males, but larger differences in wages than in marginal productivity, and thus suggests discrimination. Also using the WECD, Hellerstein *et al.* (2002) find that among manufacturing plants with high product market power, those employing more women are more profitable, again consistent with discrimination. Hersch (1991a) shows that law suits, decisions, and settlements have a substantial impact on the value of firms involved in discrimination litigation, with the drop in firm value far greater than average direct costs of settling the case. This suggests that such firms will be required to make costly changes in employment practices and is thus consistent with a discriminatory environment prior to litigation.

In the following I discuss several studies which have information on actual productivity as well as on earnings. Although such information is available only in narrow occupations, which necessarily limits generality, such studies add important information to understanding pay disparities.

One notable study that examines discrimination in hiring is by Goldin and Rouse (2000). Many orchestras started using blind auditions in the 1970s and 1980s, in which the auditioning musician would perform behind a screen. Goldin and Rouse find that the share of female musicians in a set of nine orchestras rose from about 10 percent in 1970 to about 20 percent in 1990. After accounting for general increases in women's labor force participation and in the share of women studying at leading music schools, as well as individual fixed effects feasible because individual musicians audition for multiple orchestras, Goldin and Rouse find somewhat mixed evidence but overall conclude that the use of screens reduces discrimination against women in orchestra hiring.

There have been many studies examining discrimination in academia. Although actual productivity embodies more than publications, publication productivity is reported in a number of data sets on academics and is doubtlessly an important determinant of earnings. For the most part, research shows little gender difference in pay within rank, but considerable differences in promotion from assistant to associate professor.

One recent example is by Ginther and Hayes (2003). This paper uses data from the Survey of Doctorate Recipients on academics with doctorates in the humanities in the 1977–1995 waves. The survey provides information on demographic characteristics, educational background, primary work activity, employer characteristics, and salary.

They analyze a cross-sectional sample of full-time tenured or tenure track faculty as well as a longitudinal sample. Salary differences are explained by differences in rank, but there are gender differences in promotion to tenure (probability and duration) controlling for experience, children, career employment patterns, field of study, and publications. Although the presence of children has a negative effect on promotion probability and duration, performing the counterfactual that women have no children has only a small effect on promotion probability and duration. There is also little support for a productivity difference by sex, as there is little difference in publication output, and the coefficients on publications are more favorable to women.

Smith (2002) examines differences among veterinarians in pay and in productivity, using data from annual wage surveys conducted in 1994 and 1995 for *Veterinary Economics*.[1] The sample includes veterinarians who report full-time employment as a private practice veterinarian and have at least one year of experience. The usual track for veterinarians is to start as employees of a practice before forming higher-paying partnerships or choosing self-employment. Female veterinarians are younger with about half the average work experience as male veterinarians, although there is little difference in hours worked per week. The unadjusted wage disparity among wage and salary veterinarians is 15 percent.

Of particular value of the *Veterinary Economics* salary survey is unique information on actual productivity (measured by annual revenue produced by each individual veterinarian, which equals the amount billed out by each individual vet for his or her practice), as well as the number of patients seen per hour. Smith finds a pay gap larger than the productivity gap. In fact, females actually have a greater increase in revenue per additional patient than do men, and the coefficients in the revenue equations show that women's measured characteristics are more favorable to producing revenue than are men's. In short, female veterinarians are not less productive than are male veterinarians, yet, nonetheless, female wage and salary veterinarians earn less than male.

[1] *Veterinary Economics* is a practitioner journal circulated free of charge to private-practice veterinarians on request.

Controls for direct measures of productivity (patients per hour, revenue produced) have little effect on the gap.

There is a substantial literature examining racial discrimination using professional athletes. Professional sports provide an attractive arena to examine discrimination because measures of productivity as well as salary are available. But such research generally is limited to examining race or ethnic gaps between productivity and salary, as most professional sports do not involve men and women competing in the same events. Thoroughbred horse racing is the only major professional sport in which men and women compete in the same events. Ray and Grimes (1993) examine whether female jockeys are less likely to have the opportunity to compete in races with bigger prizes, controlling for productivity as measured by win record as well as for age and apprenticeship status. They find that female jockeys secured 48 percent fewer stakes race mounts than male jockeys. Controlling for number of mounts as well as for win record, male jockeys with better win records earn more, but winnings of female jockeys is unaffected by their win record. This finding suggests that female jockeys are not competing against men in high-stake races and is consistent with discrimination against female jockeys in entry to higher purse races.

10

Concluding Comments

Women earn less than men, and no matter how extensively regressions control for market characteristics, working conditions, individual characteristics, children, housework time, and observed productivity, an unexplained gender pay gap remains for all but the most inexperienced of workers. If the unexplained pay disparity sometimes favored women and sometimes favored men, there would be no reason for concern. Unexplained residuals are a fact of life in regression analysis. But systematically and without exception finding that women earn less than men raises some questions. What unobserved something is it that cannot be measured, is correlated with sex, and explains more of a pay disparity than known determinants of earnings such as education and experience? Coupled with recent class action sex discrimination litigation involving the securities industry, grocery stores, and now Wal-Mart, it is hard to continue to attribute the remaining disparity to unmeasurables and intangibles like effort and motivation and to ignore the possibility that discrimination remains a factor in the gender pay disparity.

References

Altonji, J. G. and R. M. Blank (1999), 'Race and gender in the labor market'. In: O. C. Ashenfelter and D. Card (eds.): *Handbook of Labor Economics*, Vol. 3. Amsterdam: Elsevier Science B.V.

Anderson, D. J., M. Binder, and K. Krause (2003), 'The motherhood wage penalty revisited: Experience, heterogeneity, work effort, and work-schedule flexibility'. *Industrial & Labor Relations Review* **56**, 273–294.

Arrow, K. J. (1973), 'The theory of discrimination'. In: O. Ashenfelter and A. Rees (eds.): *Discrimination in Labor Markets.* New Jersey: Princeton University Press.

Ashraf, J. (1996), 'Is gender pay discrimination on the wane? Evidence from panel data, 1968–1989'. *Industrial & Labor Relations Review* **49**, 537–546.

Barnes, W. F. and E. B. Jones (1974), 'Differences in male and female quitting'. *Journal of Human Resources* **9**, 439–451.

Bayard, K., J. Hellerstein, D. Neumark, and K. Troske (2003), 'New evidence on sex segregation and sex differences in wages from matched employee-employer data'. *Journal of Labor Economics* **21**, 887–922.

Becker, G. S. (1957), *The Economics of Discrimination.* Illinois: University of Chicago Press.

Bergmann, B. (1974), 'Occupational segregation, wages, and profits when employers discriminate by race or sex'. *Eastern Economic Journal* **1**, 103–110.

Black, S. E. and E. Brainerd (2004), 'Importing equality? The impact of globalization on gender discrimination'. *Industrial & Labor Relations Review* **57**, 540–559.

Blau, F. D. (1977), *Equal Pay in the Office*. Massachusetts: Lexington Books.

Blau, F. D. and L. M. Kahn (1981), 'Race and sex differentials in quits by young workers'. *Industrial & Labor Relations Review* **34**, 563–577.

Blau, F. D. and L. M. Kahn (1997), 'Swimming upstream: Trends in the gender wage differential in the 1980s'. *Journal of Labor Economics* **15**, 1–42.

Blinder, A. (1973), 'Wage discrimination: Reduced form and structural estimates'. *Journal of Human Resources* **8**, 436–455.

Bonke, J., N. D. Gupta, and N. Smith (2003), 'Timing and flexibility of housework and men and women's wages'. IZA Discussion Paper No. 860.

Boraas, S. and W. M. Rodgers III (2003), 'How does gender play a role in the earnings gap? An update'. *Monthly Labor Review* **126**, 9–15.

Bowlus, A. J. (1997), 'A search interpretation of male–female wage differentials'. *Journal of Labor Economics* **15**, 625–657.

Breen, R. and C. García-Peñalosa (2002), 'Bayesian learning and gender segregation'. *Journal of Labor Economics* **20**, 899–922.

Brown, C. and M. Corcoran (1997), 'Sex-based differences in school content and male–female wage gap'. *Journal of Labor Economics* **15**, 431–465.

Budig, M. J. and P. England (2001), 'The wage penalty for motherhood'. *American Sociological Review* **66**, 204–225.

Coverman, S. (1983), 'Gender, domestic labor time, and wage inequality'. *American Sociological Review* **48**, 623–637.

DeLeire, T. and H. Levy (2004), 'Worker sorting and the risk of death on the job'. *Journal of Labor Economics* **22**, 925–953.

England, P. (1982), 'The failure of human capital theory to explain occupational sex segregation'. *Journal of Human Resources* **17**, 358–370.

Fishback, P. V. and J. V. Terza (1989), 'Are estimates of sex discrimination by employers robust? The use of never-marrieds'. *Economic Inquiry* **27**, 271–285.

Fortin, N. M. and T. Lemieux (1998), 'Rank regressions, wage distributions, and the gender gap'. *Journal of Human Resources* **33**, 610–643.

Gariety, B. S. and S. Shaffer (2001), 'Wage differentials associated with flextime'. *Monthly Labor Review* **124**, 68–75.

Ginther, D. K. and K. J. Hayes (2003), 'Gender differences in salary and promotion for faculty in the humanities 1977–1995'. *Journal of Human Resources* **38**, 34–73.

Goldin, C. (1997), 'Career and family: College women look to the past'. In: F. D. Blau and R. G. Ehrenberg (eds.): *Gender & Family Issues in the Workplace.* New York: Russell Sage Foundation.

Goldin, C. and C. Rouse (2000), 'Orchestrating impartiality: The impact of "Blind" auditions on female musicians'. *The American Economic Review* **90**, 715–741.

Groshen, E. (1991), 'The structure of the female/male wage differential: is it who you are, what you do, or where you work?'. *Journal of Human Resources* **26**, 457–472.

Heckman, J. J. (1979), 'Sample selection bias as a specification error'. *Econometrica* **47**, 153–161.

Hellerstein, J. K., D. Neumark, and K. R. Troske (1999), 'Wages, productivity, and worker characteristics: Evidence from plant-level production functions and wage equations'. *Journal of Labor Economics* **17**, 409–446.

Hellerstein, J. K., D. Neumark, and K. R. Troske (2002), 'Market forces and sex discrimination'. *Journal of Human Resources* **37**, 353–380.

Hersch, J. (1985), 'Effect of housework on earnings of husbands and wives: Evidence from full-time piece rate workers'. *Social Science Quarterly* **66**, 210–217.

Hersch, J. (1991a), 'Equal employment opportunity law and firm profitability'. *Journal of Human Resources* **26**, 139–153.

Hersch, J. (1991b), 'The impact of nonmarket work on market wages'. *American Economic Review* **81**, 157–160.

Hersch, J. (1991c), 'Male–female differences in hourly wages: The role of human capital, working conditions, and housework'. *Industrial & Labor Relations Review* **44**, 746–759.

Hersch, J. (1996), 'Smoking, seat belts, and other risky consumer decisions: Differences by gender and race'. *Managerial and Decision Economics* **17**, 471–481.

Hersch, J. (1998), 'Compensating differentials for gender-specific job injury risks'. *American Economic Review* **88**, 598–607.

Hersch, J. (2003), 'The new labor market for lawyers: Will female lawyers still earn less?'. *Cardozo Women's Law Journal* **10**, 1–59.

Hersch, J. and P. Reagan (1997), 'Worker effort decisions and efficient gender-specific wage-tenure profiles'. *Economic Inquiry* **35**, 193–207.

Hersch, J. and L. S. Stratton (1997), 'Housework, fixed effects, and wages of married workers'. *Journal of Human Resources* **32**, 285–307.

Hersch, J. and L. S. Stratton (2002), 'Housework and wages'. *Journal of Human Resources* **37**, 218–229.

Hill, M. S. (1979), 'The wage effects of marital status and children'. *Journal of Human Resources* **14**, 579–594.

Hundley, G. (2000), 'Male/female earnings differences in self-employment: The effects of marriage, children, and the household division of labor'. *Industrial & Labor Relations Review* **54**, 95–114.

Jacobsen, J. P., J. W. Pearce III, and J. L. Rosenbloom (1999), 'The effects of child-bearing on married women's labor supply and earnings: Using twin births as a natural experiment'. *Journal of Human Resources* **34**, 449–474.

Jianakoplos, N. A. and A. Bernasek (1998), 'Are women more risk averse?'. *Economic Inquiry* **36**, 620–630.

Juhn, C., K. M. Murphy, and B. Pierce (1991), 'Accounting for the slowdown in black–white wage convergence'. University Press of America.

Juhn, C., K. M. Murphy, and B. Pierce (1993), 'Wage inequality and the rise in returns to skill'. *Journal of Political Economy* **101**, 410–442.

Keith, K. and P. Malone (2005), 'Housework and the wages of young, middle-aged, and older workers'. *Contemporary Economic Policy* **23**, 224–241.

Keith, K. and A. McWilliams (1995), 'The wage effects of cumulative job mobility'. *Industrial & Labor Relations Review* **49**, 121–137.

Keith, K. and A. McWilliams (1997), 'Job mobility and gender-based wage growth differentials'. *Economic Inquiry* **35**, 320–333.

Keith, K. and A. McWilliams (1999), 'The returns to mobility and job search by gender'. *Industrial & Labor Relations Review* **52**, 460–477.

Korenman, S. and D. Neumark (1992), 'Marriage, motherhood, and wages'. *Journal of Human Resources* **27**, 233–255.

Leeth, J. D. and J. Ruser (2003), 'Compensating wage differentials for fatal and nonfatal injury risk by gender and race'. *The Journal of Risk and Uncertainty* **27**, 257–277.

Lemieux, T. (2006), 'Increasing residual wage inequality: Composition effects, noisy data, or rising demand for skill?'. *American Economic Review* **96**, 461–498.

Light, A. and M. Ureta (1992), 'Panel estimates of male and female job turnover behavior: Can female nonquitters be identified?'. *Journal of Labor Economics* **10**, 156–181.

Lundberg, S. and E. Rose (2000), 'Parenthood and the earnings of married men and women'. *Labour Economics* **7**, 689–710.

Macpherson, D. A. and B. T. Hirsch (1995), 'Wages and gender composition: Why do women's jobs pay less?'. *Journal of Labor Economics* **13**, 426–471.

Manski, C. F. (1989), 'Anatomy of the selection problem'. *Journal of Human Resources* **24**, 343–360.

Mincer, J. and S. Polachek (1974), 'Family investments in human capital: earnings of women'. *Journal of Political Economy* **82**, S76–S108.

Mortensen, D. (1990), 'Equilibrium wage distributions: A synthesis'. In: J. Hartog, G. Ridder, and J. Theeuwes (eds.): *Panel Data and Labour Market Studies*. North Holland, Amsterdam.

Neumark, D. (1988), 'Employers' discriminatory behavior and the estimation of wage discrimination'. *Journal of Human Resources* **23**, 279–295.

Neumark, D. and S. Korenman (1994), 'Sources of bias in women's wage equations: Results using sibling data'. *Journal of Human Resources* **29**, 379–405.

Noonan, M. (2001), 'The impact of domestic work on men's and women's wages'. *Journal of Marriage and the Family* **63**, 1134–1145.

Oaxaca, R. (1973), 'Male–female wage differentials in urban labor markets'. *International Economic Review* **14**, 693–709.

O'Neill, J. E. and D. M. O'Neill (2005), "What do wage differentials tell us about labor market discrimination?", Working Paper No. 11240. National Bureau of Economic Research.

Paglin, M. and A. M. Rufolo (1990), 'Heterogeneous human capital, occupational choice, and male–female earnings differences'. *Journal of Labor Economics* **8**, 123–145.

Phelps, E. S. (1972), 'The statistical theory of racism and sexism'. *American Economic Review* **62**, 659–661.

Phipps, S., P. Burton, and L. Lethbridge (2001), 'In and out of the labour market: Long term income consequences of child-related interruptions to women's paid work'. *Canadian Journal of Economics* **34**, 411–429.

Polachek, S. W. (1975a), 'Differences in expected post-school investment as a determinant of market wage differentials'. *International Economic Review* **16**, 451–470.

Polachek, S. W. (1975b), 'Potential biases in measuring male–female discrimination'. *Journal of Human Resources* **10**, 205–229.

Polachek, S. W. (1978), 'Sex differences in college major'. *Industrial & Labor Relations Review* **31**, 498–508.

Polachek, S. W. (1981), 'Occupational self-selection: A human capital approach to sex differences in occupational structure'. *Review of Economics and Statistics* **73**, 60–69.

Ray, M. A. and P. W. Grimes (1993), 'Jockeying for position: Winnings and gender discrimination on the thoroughbred racetrack'. *Social Science Quarterly* **74**, 46–61.

Reskin, B. F. and D. D. Bielby (2005), 'A sociological perspective on gender and career outcomes'. *Journal of Economic Perspectives* **19**, 71–86.

Robst, J. and J. VanGilder (2000), 'Atrophy rates in male and female occupations'. *Economics Letters* **69**, 407–413.

Royalty, A. B. (1998), 'Job-to-job and job-to-nonemployment turnover by gender and education level'. *Journal of Labor Economics* **16**, 392–443.

Sandell, S. H. and D. Shapiro (1980), 'Work expectations, human capital accumulation, and the wages of young women'. *Journal of Human Resources* **15**, 335–353.

Sasser, A. C. (2005), 'Gender differences in physician pay: Trade-offs between career and family'. *Journal of Human Resources* **40**, 477–504.

Shelton, B. A. and J. Firestone (1989), 'Household labor time and the gender gap in earnings'. *Gender and Society* **3**, 105–112.

Sicherman, N. (1996), 'Gender differences in departures from a large firm'. *Industrial & Labor Relations Review* **49**, 484–505.

Smith, D. M. (2002), 'Pay and productivity differences between male and female veterinarians'. *Industrial & Labor Relations Review* **55**, 493–511.

Stratton, L. S. (2001), 'Why does more housework lower women's wages? Testing hypotheses involving job effort and hours flexibility'. *Social Science Quarterly* **82**, 67–76.

Suen, W. (1997), 'Decomposing wage residuals: Unmeasured skill or statistical artifact?'. *Journal of Labor Economics* **15**, 555–566.

The College Board, available at www.collegeboard.com/prod_downloads/about/news_info/cbsenior/yr2002/pdf/table2.pdf.

Turner, S. E. and W. G. Bowen (1999), 'Choice of major: the changing (unchanging) gender gap'. *Industrial & Labor Relations Review* **52**, 289–313.

U.S. Department of Education, National Center for Education Statistics (2004), 'Digest of Education Statistics 2003'. http://nces.ed.gov/pubs2005/2005025.pdf.

U.S. Department of Labor, Bureau of Labor Statistics (2004), 'Number of Jobs Held, Labor Market Activity, and Earnings Growth Among Younger Baby Boomers: Recent Results from a Longitudinal Survey'. National Longitudinal Survey of Youth 1979, http://www.bls.gov/news.release/pdf/nlsoy.pdf.

U.S. Department of Labor, Bureau of Labor Statistics (2004), 'Employee Tenure in 2004'. www.bls.gov/news.release/pdf/tenure.pdf.

U.S. Department of Labor, Bureau of Labor Statistics (2005), 'Highlights of Women's Earnings in 2004'. Report 987. http://www.bls.gov/cps/cpswom2004.pdf.

U.S. Department of Labor, Bureau of Labor Statistics (2005). Report 985. http://www.bls.gov/cps/wlf-databook-2005.pdf.

U.S. Department of Labor, Bureau of Labor Statistics (2005), 'Workers in Flexible and Shift Schedules in May 2004'. http://www.bls.gov/news.release/pdf/flex.pdf.

U.S. Department of Labor, Bureau of Labor Statistics (2005), 'American Time Use Survey — 2004 Results Announced by BLS'. www.bls.gov/tus.

U.S. Department of Labor, Bureau of Labor Statistics, Census of Fatal Occupational Injuries (2004). http://www.bls.gove/iif/oshwc/cfoi/cftb0202.pdf.

U.S. Department of Labor, Bureau of Labor Statistics (2005), 'Workplace Injuries and Illnesses in 2004'. http://www.bls.gov/news.release/pdf/osh2.pdf.

U.S. Department of Labor, Women in the Labor Force: A Databook, (2005). http://www.bls.gov/cps/wlf-databook2006.htm.

Viscusi, W. K. (1980), 'Sex differences in worker quitting'. *Review of Economics and Statistics* **62**, 388–397.

Waldfogel, J. (1997a), 'The effect of children on women's wages'. *American Sociological Review* **62**, 209–217.

Waldfogel, J. (1997b), 'Working mothers then and now: A cross-cohort analysis of the effects of maternity leave on women's pay'. In: F. D. Blau and R. G. Ehrenberg (eds.): *Gender & Family Issues in the Workplace*. New York: Russell Sage Foundation.

Waldfogel, J. (1998), 'The family gap for young women in the United States and Britain: Can maternity leave make a difference?'. *Journal of Labor Economics* **16**, 505–545.

Weinberger, C. J. (1999), 'Mathematical college majors and the gender gap in wages'. *Industrial Relations* **38**.

Recommended Reading

Blau, F. D., M. Ferber, and A. Winkler (2001), *The Economics of Women, Men, and Work.* New Jersey: Prentice Hall.

Blau, F. D. (1998), 'Trends in the well-being of American women, 1970–1995'. *Journal of Economic Literature* **36**, 112–165.

Cain, G. G. (1986), 'The economic analysis of labor market discrimination: a survey'. In: O. C. Ashenfelter and R. Layard (eds.): *Handbook of Labor Economics*, Vol. 1. Amsterdam: North Holland.

Goldin, C. (1990), *Understanding the Gender Gap.* New York: Oxford University Press.

Polachek, S. W. (2004), 'How the human capital model explains why the gender wage gap narrowed'. *Discussion Paper No. 1102*, Forschungsinstitut zur Zukunft der Arbeit/Institute for the Study of Labor (IZA).

Sorensen, E. (1991), *Exploring the Reasons behind the Narrowing Gender Gap in Earnings.* Washington, DC: Urban Institute.

Breinigsville, PA USA
30 December 2010
252459BV00003B/29/A

9 781933 019475